Changed Imagination, Changed Obedience

Changed Imagination, Changed Obedience

Social Imagination and the Bent-Over Woman
in the Gospel of Luke

NATALIE K. HOUGHTBY-HADDON

PICKWICK *Publications* · Eugene, Oregon

CHANGED IMAGINATION, CHANGED OBEDIENCE
Social Imagination and the Bent-Over Woman in the Gospel of Luke

Pickwick Publications
An Imprint of Wipf and Stock Publishers
199 W. 8th Ave., Suite 3
Eugene, OR 97401

www.wipfandstock.com

ISBN 13: 978-1-60899-675-9

Cataloging-in-Publication data:

Houghtby-Haddon, Natalie K.

Changed imagination, changed obedience : social imagination and the bent-over woman in the gospel of Luke / Natalie K. Houghtby-Haddon.

xx + 170 p. ; 23 cm. Includes bibliographical references and index.

ISBN 13: 978-1-60899-675-9

1. Bible. N.T. Luke—Criticism, interpretation, etc. 2. Women in the Bible. 3. Slavery in the Bible. 4. Organizational change.

BS2595.2 H6 2011

Manufactured in the U.S.A.

For Harlan and Phyllis Houghtby
and
In Memory of Dick

———•———

He has told you, O Man, what is good,
And what does the Lord require of you?
To make justice,
To love mercy,
And to travel humbly with your God.

—Micah 6:8 (LXX)

Contents

Figures

Tables

Acknowledgments

S INCE THIS BOOK BEGAN life as my PhD dissertation, let me first thank Professor Paul B. Duff, who in 2001 agreed over a cup of coffee to be my dissertation advisor, a role I am sure he never thought would take as long as it did, in order for me to finally finish. Since he signed on, he has consumed more cups of coffee than anyone should be expected to drink, read more versions of various parts of the story of the Bent-Over Woman than anyone should have to read, and has been unfailingly teacher, mentor, colleague, and friend. His careful reading of my dissertation, and its transformation into this book, has improved the text you hold in your hands immeasurably.

I also owe a tremendous debt of gratitude to Mr. Jim Robinson, Executive Director of The George Washington University Center for Excellence in Public Leadership. Jim has been extraordinarily gracious in making it possible for me to carve out writing time from my responsibilities for the Center, not only to finish my dissertation, but also to transform it into this book. His imaginative and collaborative leadership style makes the Center a wonderful place to work, and his mentoring has helped us all to reach more of our potential, not only as public leaders, but also as human beings in the world. I aspire to be a leader like him.

I also owe a debt of gratitude to the staff of the Center. Their willingness to pitch in as needed on all the leadership programs sponsored by the Center makes it easy for us to be successful, and has made it possible for me to take time to write, knowing that the work of the Center was in extremely capable hands. I especially want to thank those who have been on the staff during the past two years and have therefore borne the brunt of my writing schedule: Karima Morris Woods, Colleen Oakes, Ina Gjikondi, and Chantal Cardon. I also want to thank my colleagues who form the core faculty team of the Center: Darrell Harvey, Frank Staroba, Roosevelt Thomas, Chris Kayes, A. J. Robinson, and Maureen Brown. They have inspired me, challenged me, and made me a better teacher and thinker. I am proud to call them friends. I also want to acknowledge two former colleagues on the Center's faculty: Matthew Fairholm and Kari Moe. They, along with Herb Tillery, the Center's then Executive Director, welcomed me onto the Center's staff in the fall of 2000, introduced me to the arcane mysteries of public administration and leadership theory, and helped me think through the various components of this project at its earliest stages.

I also need to express my profound gratitude to Megan Davis, who entered the GW PhD Program in the Human Sciences at the same time as I did. Megan has been my teaching partner, collaborating with me on our course in Marx and Faith, and on the many semesters of Introduction to the New Testament I have taught for the University. In company with our students, she has lived through the various iterations of the Social Imagination model, helping me to make it clearer and more usable each time I work with it in my classes. She also made me aware of the discipline of disabilities studies through her own scholarship, so that I owe a considerable section of the thought-world of this study to her guidance. Megan has taught me how to think more critically, to argue more thoughtfully, and to look at the world with a more nuanced understanding of the barriers to justice faced by many "invisible" people.

I also thank the hundreds of students in my New Testament and World Religion classes at GW who have applied various forms of the Social Imagination model to their analysis of New Testament texts and contemporary social issues over the years. Their insights, evaluations, and critiques have made the model a much more effective tool for understanding how religion and sacred texts embody the social imagination of communities in various places and times throughout history.

I am also grateful to my friend Allison Taylor, who graciously brought a fresh pair of eyes to this project, reading the book manuscript from cover to cover, and helping me to clarify various points that I had glossed over through too much familiarity with the subject. She, along with Paul Duff, should be excused from any errors that remain, which are solely my responsibility.

The reader will soon discover that I owe my biggest debt of gratitude to Burton L. Mack, Professor Emeritus of Early Christianity at the Claremont School of Theology. In January of 1983, I walked into his course on "the Passion Narrative in the Gospel of Mark" at CST, and the world has never been the same for me. Professor Mack opened the world of the New Testament texts to me in a way that gave voice to my experience of them, and gave me a map for exploring them. He has been unfailing in his generosity as teacher, as mentor, and as friend, including sharing with me the manuscript of his Gap Theory when I was working on my Doctor of Ministry dissertation. Knowing I had not done it justice in that work, I hope that its transformation into the Social Imagination model that forms the basis of my work in this study is a better representation of its power to help social groups negotiate competing values as they seek to live together in a way that is healthy, just, and sustainable.

This book is dedicated to my parents, Harlan and Phyllis Houghtby, and to my late husband, the Rev. Richard P. Houghtby-Haddon. Their lives and ministries have been an unfailing witness to God's expectation that doing justice, loving kindness, and walking humbly with God are possible, while their love for me has been an unmediated experience of God's grace in my life.

Preface

ONCE UPON A TIME, there was a United Methodist congregation in Southern California who welcomed a young woman as the new pastor in their midst. The young woman had been told by her District Superintendent that the congregation had agreed to participate in a pilot program for congregational development—what in the world of organizational development is called organizational change. The young pastor was excited; changing organizations to make them better was what she loved to do. And so she leaped into the task with great energy and enthusiasm, but was soon confused and dismayed by the resistance of the congregation to this great new vision of the kind of church they could be. Why didn't they see the future she could see for them? Why couldn't they imagine the great alternative life she could give them, if only they would do what she told them to do? Why didn't they just trust her? After all, she was the Pastor-in-Charge, wasn't she? She was the one appointed by the Bishop to lead the congregation—so why didn't they follow her?

As the reader has probably surmised, I was that young pastor, and that congregation was only the first of several groups that bore the brunt of my well-intentioned, but not very skillful attempts at helping organizations change in order to move into a more vital future for themselves. In those days, "change leadership" was not yet a concept in the business section of bookstores, John Kotter had yet to write about his eight stages of change,[1] and William Bridges' work in managing transitions was still way over the horizon for me.[2] Church administration was barely given a nod in my seminary training, and organizational behavior and development were concepts I was not to hear much about for more than another decade—and then not in the context of church leadership.

But the church is, at its core, predicated on the notion of change, change that happens at two levels: personal change, as an individual com-

1. Kotter, *Leading Change*.
2. Bridges, *Managing Transitions*.

mits her or his life to Jesus Christ and begins to live in a new way, and social change, as Christians work together as the Church, the Body of Christ, to make God's kingdom real through changed societies in which the hungry are fed, the naked are clothed, captives are released, and the oppressed go free. Why, then, was it so hard for the congregations that I pastored—and other organizations with which I have worked since—to make the changes that would have helped them move into a sustainable, vibrant future?

It was not until I was President of Immaculate Heart College Center (IHCC) in Los Angeles, and the Board of Trustees and I had come to the very painful conclusion that the best future for the Center was to close, that I began to have a glimmer of what might lie behind the inability to make the necessary changes that would have prevented the closure of the school. The decision to close came after three years of grappling with possible alternatives for improving IHCC's financial position. What finally began to dawn on me towards the end of that time was that the majority of the Board members, who were long-time members of the Immaculate Heart Community and, in many cases, graduates of the College, quite literally could not see that the suggestions I and another Board member made for different fund raising strategies might be possible to implement. This Board member and I were the only two persons on the Board who came from outside the IHM community, and in fact, came from outside Roman Catholicism; until this experience, I had not really understood the power of our past experiences to limit the range of options we could cognitively conceptualize.

As I reflected on this failed change effort, and on those that had come before in several of the congregations I had served, I began to realize that an inability to imagine an alternative future lay at the heart of our inability to change. Perhaps as importantly, it was the inability to imagine a future that would respect and honor the past, instead of simply move into the future as some unrecognizable new entity, which created resistance and resentment about proposed changes.

So began my quest to find some way to help people imagine their lives—and the lives of the organizations of which they were a part—differently. I realized that I already had a few pieces of the puzzle in hand. The first piece came from Walter Brueggemann, who at the 1989 Ministers' Convocation at the Claremont School of Theology quoted Paul Ricoeur as saying that "changed obedience follows changed imagination."

While the quotation had stuck with me, it was not until I reflected on my experiences of failed change efforts at Immaculate Heart ten years later that I realized the full import of what Ricoeur was saying: that people don't/won't, in fact, *can't* change what they do (obedience) until they have changed their imaginations and can see for themselves that there is some other possible way of acting. At that same lecture, Brueggemann also described Sabbath rest as the opportunity to imagine one's life differently, and so the idea of Sabbath and Sabbath rest became a second piece of the puzzle.[3] The next pieces of the puzzle came to me a couple of years later as I wrote my Doctor of Ministry dissertation at Claremont. The first in this set of puzzle pieces was Jonathan Z. Smith's proposal that social change is a function of symbol change, which served as the conceptual framework undergirding my dissertation.[4] The second piece was Burton L. Mack's "Gap Theory" of preaching, which he shared with me and encouraged me to use as part of my dissertation research;[5] it is this theory that has been transformed into the Social Imagination model that forms the basis for the present study. The third piece was the inclusion of the Bent-Over-Woman story from the Gospel of Luke as one of the women whose stories I analyzed as part of my research.[6] What didn't strike me at that time, but became clear to me later, was that her story was a story that could be understood as an example of Brueggemann's proposal that Sabbath is an opportunity to imagine one's own life—as well as the life of the community—differently, which is really the whole point of the Sabbath controversy stories in the gospels, it seems to me.

The final pieces of the puzzle came to me through my work as the Associate Director of The George Washington University Center for Excellence in Public Leadership, and as a doctoral student at GW, first in public policy, and then in the human sciences. In preparing to teach leadership theory for the Center, I at last was introduced to organizational behavior and development, and the various theories of change management and leadership that I wish I had known when I was a local church pastor. The educational theory that forms the foundation for the Center's leadership development programs is David Kolb's Experiential Learning

3. Brueggemann, "Restlessness and Greed."

4. Smith, "Influence of Symbols on Social Change," 129–46.

5. Mack, "The Gospel and the Gaps."

6. Houghtby, "Living Beyond the Horizon," 43–49.

Theory (ELT), which is a four-stage cycle of experience, reflection, thinking, and acting;[7] this is the way in which adults learn best, according to Kolb. Through my research in public policy, I was introduced to participatory and discursive democracy, forms of governance and public policy formation that involve citizens, and not just technical experts, in the development of policy responses to the issues confronting a community or society.[8] My work in the human sciences completed the puzzle, introducing me to Pierre Bourdieu's concept of the *habitus*,[9] which, it turned out, was what I had run aground on at Immaculate Heart. I also learned the tools of interdisciplinary research and reflection, which have provided me with the ability to see the disparate pieces of my quest as part of a single pattern, diverse and textured though it may be.

This study presents the findings of my quest, which culminated in my PhD dissertation at GW. Chapter 1 lays out the conceptual framework that structures the study. I begin with Bourdieu's *habitus*, and then move on to explore myth as part of the symbol system that sustains the *habitus*. Jonathan Z. Smith's proposal that symbol change can result in social change becomes the next stage of my exploration, which is completed by the development of the Social Imagination model as the primary tool for analysis and construction to be used throughout the study. In chapters 2, 3, and 4, I apply the Social Imagination model to the analysis of a text from the Gospel of Luke, the story of the Bent-Over Woman in Luke 13:10–17. My argument is that this story serves as an interpretive key for understanding how Luke's social vision for his community is revealed over the course of the Gospel and Acts, and that it is, in essence, a proposal by Luke for how the community could imagine its life differently. In chapter 5, I return to the present, in order to show how contemporary social groups might use the Social Imagination model to construct a process that enables them to think together about how to respond to critical issues confronting them.

My hope is that this study of how the social imagination informs social change will provide a framework that can be used by groups and individuals who sense that something needs to be changed in their congregations, neighborhoods, or organizations if they are to have a vibrant,

---

7. Kolb and Kolb, "Learning Styles and Learning Spaces," 194.

8. Dryzek, *Discursive Democracy*.

9. Bourdieu, *The Logic of Practice*.

sustainable future, but do not know where or how to begin. Forming the background to this exploration is my vocation as both preacher and biblical scholar, one whose professional life has been grounded in the presumption that conversation matters, that texts serve as the source of imagination, possibility, and expectation about how a community should organize its life together, and that change is not only possible, but anticipated—both for individuals and for the communities to which they belong—because of an ongoing conversation that takes place among the community and its members, its foundational texts, and the world in which it finds itself. It is this conversation that will be the substance of the study. So I think I have at least a partial answer to my quest for how individuals and groups can imagine their lives differently—together. Shall we begin? Once upon a time . . .

1

Myths and Worlds

The "Stuff" of Social Change

INTRODUCTION

THIS STUDY IS THE result of my search to find an answer to the question, "How do we create healthy, just, and sustainable communities?" What I have discovered over the years from my work with a variety of organizations is that a better way to pose the question is to ask, "How can we *imagine* what healthy, just, and sustainable communities look like? . . . and then what do we do to create them?" For my experience has been that the ability to imagine alternative ways of living together, whether in a church, an academic institution, a neighborhood, or the community of nations, is hard to do, and is largely dependent on the ability of those who make up a given social group to imagine alternative possibilities for how they might structure their life together. Therefore, in this chapter I explore some of the obstacles to imagination, and then develop a model of the social imagination that may help a social group overcome those obstacles.

I begin with a discussion of Pierre Bourdieu's *habitus*, proposing that it is a social group's mythic system which undergirds the stability of the *habitus* over time. I then look at instances when a mythic system changes inadvertently, and suggest that one might work proactively to change such a system in order to promote intended, rather than accidental, social change. I conclude this chapter with the exploration of the Social Imagination model, which will then serve as our tool for analysis and development for the remainder of the study.

MYTHIC SYMBOL SYSTEMS AND THE CREATION
OF COMMUNITY

Pierre Bourdieu has noted the critical importance of the use of all kinds of symbols in the construction and maintenance of a society. He asserts, "Symbols are the instrument par excellence of 'social integration': as instruments of knowledge and communication . . . they make it possible for there to be a *consensus* on the meaning of the social world, a consensus which contributes fundamentally to the reproduction of the social order."[1] Thus, for any given social group's "world" to be maintained, there must be a symbol system that carries shared meaning for each member of the group. As the group members seek to make sense of their lives—to give meaning to that which they encounter and what they experience—they use the structures of meaning available to them from their social context. The mythical, religious, political, and ideological frameworks that help persons structure meaning are elements of the social world that are generally taken for granted, enabling persons to move back and forth seamlessly between their current experience and the symbolic frameworks they use to give that experience meaning. Peter Berger describes the "naturalizing" of these frameworks as a three-stage process using *externalization*, "the ongoing outpouring of human being into the world, both in the physical and the mental activity of men"; *objectivation*, "attainment by the products of this activity of a reality that confronts its producers as a facticity external to and other than themselves"; and *internalization*, "the re-appropriation by men of this same reality, transforming it once again from the structures of the objective world into structures of the subjective consciousness."[2] This process is interactive, so that a group of persons come together to form a society, which then shapes them and their descendents, who, as they accept, reject, and add elements to the social world reshape society, which shapes them and their descendents, who reshape society as they accept, reject, and add elements to the social world, which shapes them . . . and so on, as long as the society exists. In this process, certain elements may remain virtually unchanged over time, while others may undergo considerable change to accommodate the changing experiences of the members of the society.

---

1. Bourdieu, *The Logic of Practice*, 166 (emphasis in original).
2. Berger, *The Sacred Canopy*, 4.

Bourdieu has named this process '*habitus*,' which includes both what people do (practices) and what they believe about who they are and why they act the way they do (symbol systems). The *habitus* is a product of the social group's history, as customs and habits are developed and then taught to succeeding generations, until these customs and habits—or practices, as Bourdieu names them—are part and parcel of the cultural fabric of the social group. This cultural fabric provides the "schemes of perception, thought and action [which] tend to guarantee the 'correctness' . . . and constancy over time"[3] of the various behavioral choices a member of the social group is likely to make in response to a given situation, without thinking twice about what to do.

Thus, if one is a native member of a given *habitus*—someone born into it—one knows, as if it is 'second nature,' how to respond to a variety of social encounters. For example, the language one uses, the particular gender roles assigned to women and men, and how one shows respect to those who are older, or who have a different social status from oneself are responses a native-born member makes "unconsciously." Bourdieu suggests that we learn these social practices without being aware that we are doing so, from the time we are raised as children. Posture, gesture, tones of voice, all contribute to raising children who can function successfully in the society's *habitus*; this immersion into the do's and don'ts of the society, without being aware that one is receiving such indoctrination, is, according to Bourdieu, "the condition for the effectiveness of all kinds of symbolic power that will subsequently be able to operate on a *habitus* predisposed to respond to them."[4] Persons not born into this *habitus*, on the other hand, must be taught these responses explicitly, or they are likely to find themselves in awkward situations, unaware of what social transgression they have committed which resulted in icy stares, snickers behind hands, or some other show of disapproval. Even with such a process of education, however, non-"native" members of a given *habitus* may never be able to experience the dispositions and structures of the *habitus* as truly "natural" or "objective"—in other words, as simply the way the world is.

The *habitus* can thus be understood as the "world" in which people live. Peter Berger's work has helped to establish the role of religion in

3. Bourdieu, *Logic of Practice*, 54.
4. Ibid., 51–52.

both world-construction and world maintenance.[5] He suggests that religion is one of the most effective means for legitimating a given social practice or world, because religion is able to place the authorizing source (i.e., God) outside the frame of normal human existence.[6] This makes it difficult to challenge the social practice or shape of the world, because one must take on the social group's belief system in order to do so. A consequence of religious legitimations, however, can be that they take on a life of their own, with significant implications for society.[7]

Marriage is an excellent example of the interplay between religion and human social construction. As the social institution that historically has secured property rights by legitimating those who are eligible to inherit property from one generation to the next, marriage has been buttressed by legal and religious provisions for millennia across virtually all human cultures. In the Christian era, legal statutes were built on the gospel injunctions against divorce (Matt 19:1–12//Mark 10:1–12), while clergy were given authority by the state to officiate at legally binding, religious marriage ceremonies.[8] Thus, the notion that marriage is "an honorable estate, instituted of God . . . signifying unto us the mystical union that exists between Christ and his church . . ."[9] was grounded in the biblical texts, and served as the basis for centuries in Western civilization for the legal ban on divorce, regardless of the state of relationship between the marriage partners.[10]

5. Berger, *The Sacred Canopy*, especially chapters 1 and 2.

6. Ibid., 32.

7. Ibid., 41.

8. An excellent reminder of the implications of entwining a specific religion with a given legal system can be seen in the scene from the film *Gandhi* in which Gandhi calls together the Muslim and Hindu men of the South African colored community to discuss how to respond to General Smuts' law, which recognized only Christian marriages as legal. Briley, *Gandhi*, directed by Richard Attenborough.

9. The United Methodist Church, "A Service of Christian Marriage II," 129.

10. Not only religious legitimation is used by societies to authorize various social practices, however; political legitimation is used to legitimate social practices as well. Whatever a given society's political process may be (e.g., divine right of kings, democracy, dictatorship), if a social practice can be said to have been approved by that process, it carries the imprimatur of political authority. When the two forms of legitimation are combined, the given social practice can be nearly impossible to transform, as the four hundred years between King Henry VIII's separation from the Catholic Church in order to divorce and the gradual acceptance of divorce for all persons in the late twentieth century—which required the transformation of political laws as well as church ritual—shows.

What gives religious legitimation its power? Is it simply that the authorizing force is "out there" somewhere, beyond the normal sphere of day-to-day human encounter? I would argue that it is because religious legitimation is grounded in the mythic system of a society, which members of a society learn from childhood as explanations for "the way the world is." Thus, the mythic system has embedded within it the explanations for why social practices exist, and why these practices are conducted in a given way. As Bruce Lincoln suggests, myths are stories that have both credibility *and* authority for the social group that subscribes to them; they also work to create the contours of the social group by evoking "the sentiments out of which society is actively constructed."[11] Furthermore, if a social change is to be lastingly successful, the mythic system that has legitimized the preceding social practice will need to change to support the new "way the world is."[12]

However, myth as a category is somewhat problematic. What is myth? Is it true? false? something in between? What role does myth play? Does it record history? Offer explanations of how the world and society came to be? Provide a charter for social roles and rankings? Serve as a symbolic representation of collective understandings of the "wholly other"? Are the meanings of myth obvious and on the surface of the story, or hidden in the structure of mythic language? Is myth a mirror of society, the libretto for a social group's rituals, or something

11. Lincoln, *Discourse and the Construction of Society*, 25. Lincoln identifies four levels of stories: fable, legend, epic, and myth. He classifies narratives into one of these four categories based on three criteria: whether the story makes a truth-claim (if not, it is a fable, if yes, it is a legend), whether such a truth claim is seen as credible by the receiving audience (if yes, it is history), and whether a story with a credible truth-claim is seen as authoritative (if yes, it is a myth). Ibid., 24–25.

12. An interesting question arises when the mythic system (represented by the religious system) is no longer passed on to the next generation as a commonly shared symbol system, because religion becomes understood primarily as a personal, individualized experience between "me and my God," rather than a communal or social experience. I was struck by the lack of cultural competence—for their own culture—exhibited by students in my undergraduate classes recently, and then realized that even as significant a recent event as September 11, 2001 is ancient history for them, since they were somewhere between 8 and 10 when it occurred. How could I then expect them to understand the importance of Martin Luther King Jr.'s "I have a dream" speech—or the allusions, biblical and cultural—that were used to create its power, since most of them have little or no religious background in their families, and their parents were likely very young or not yet born in 1963?

else? Does a myth describe universal human experience, or is it culturally circumscribed?

Even more problematic a category is mythmaking itself. Who actually "makes" a myth? Can an individual? Or does it happen collectively
by some mysterious process of unconscious mutual agreement on the
contours of the story by the members of a given social group? All of
these questions make clear the challenges one faces when one contends
that one must change the sustaining mythic symbol system in order to
engage successfully in long-lasting social change. So what, then, can we
say about myth—and myth-making?

Wendy Doniger offers a rather concise understanding of myth, in
which she suggests that a myth is a narrative that is told over and over
again in a variety of settings, and that it is "transparent to a variety of
constructions of meaning" so that it is possible to hold conflicting meanings "in a charged tension." She goes on to say, "This transparency . . .
allows a myth, more than other forms of narrative, to be shared by a
group (who, as individuals, have various points of view) and to survive
through time (through different generations with different points of
view)."[13] Furthermore, she notes that Claude Levi-Strauss's notion of
bricolage is a good metaphor for describing the myth-making process,
in that

> If you take an early story (more precisely, a story that was record-
> ed early, since no one knows when it was first told) and compare
> it with later tellings, it is as if the first story was dropped and bro-
> ken into pieces, then put together again differently—not wrongly,
> just differently. The broken pieces are the atomic units of a myth.
> . . . In the ecology of narratives, recycling is a very old process
> indeed. Myths, like all things in constant use, such as Truth in the
> Midrash, get broken and fixed again, lost and found, and the one
> who finds and fixes them, the handyman who recycles them, is
> what Levi-Strauss calls a *bricoleur* . . .[14]

For example, one can imagine the gospel writers as *bricoleurs*, especially
Matthew and Luke, who have a text of Mark, and of their common
source material, Q, and the Septuagint, along with other individual material; even with the large amount of shared common material, they put
together their versions of the "Life" of Jesus in two very different ways.

13. Doniger, *The Implied Spider*, 80.
14. Ibid., 145.

Burton L. Mack has done extensive work exploring the relationship between social interests, myth-making, and social formations that are created and maintained through the interaction of these human activities. Of particular interest for this study is his discussion of how the relationship between social interests and myth-making results in "authorizing" or legitimating particular social formations.[15] Mack defines "social interest" as the "unconscious interest humans take and have taken in the collective construction of their societies."[16] This "unconscious interest" creates a mentality in which members of any given society agree to live together in particular ways, taking those agreements for granted without any explicit realization that such agreements have been negotiated collectively. Among the aspects of social organization Mack identifies as social interests are: collective understandings regarding territory and land, ancestors, the people who belong (and do not belong), rites of passage, forms of production, and social structures such as language, kinship, tuition (education), systems of exchange, rules of etiquette, and social status and position.[17]

Jonathan Z. Smith has suggested that myth is able to function as an imaginative space in which thinking takes place because it is a "self-conscious category mistake" in which the incongruity of fit (situational incongruity) between an element in a myth and a real world situation is structured in such a way that the play between the two "gives rise to thought."[18] This malleability of myth, and its ability to communicate meaning across different contexts and social conditions, suggests that the person who can tell the mythic story in a new way, or articulate a different interpretation of it, has the opportunity to reframe a social group's experience. Furthermore, the storyteller may also be creating an alternative future for the group, as they experience the mythic symbol system in a new and different way.

Bruce Lincoln has picked up on this aspect of myth, noting that myth is a form of discourse that has been used "not only for the replication of established social forms . . . but more broadly for the construction,

---

15. Mack, *Myth and the Christian Nation*, 76–81.

16. Ibid. 75.

17. Ibid., 52–73. We shall see that these are the same interests that appear to be at stake for Luke's audience.

18. Smith, "Map is Not Territory," 299–300.

deconstruction, and reconstruction of society itself."[19] He contends that such discourse offers opportunities for ideological persuasion, and can "mystify the inevitable inequities of any social order and ... win the consent of those over whom power is exercised, thereby obviating the need for the direct coercive use of force and transforming simple power into 'legitimate' authority." However, mythic discourse "can also serve members of subordinate classes in their attempts to demystify, de-legitimate, and deconstruct the established norms, institutions, and discourses that play a role in constructing their subordination."[20] Lincoln offers a further role for discourse that is helpful for thinking about myth-making as a tool for social change:

> all the tensions, contradictions, superficial stability, and potential fluidity of any given society as a whole are present within the full range of thought and discourse that circulates at any given moment. Change comes not when groups or individuals use "knowledge" to challenge ideological mystification, *but rather when they employ thought and discourse, including even such modes as myth and ritual,* as effective instruments of struggle. [21]

As these authors have pointed out, myth is a fluid social structure that is able to sustain a given social group over time because it both retains and transforms its shape as it is told and retold in response to the social group's present experience. Myth-making is thus primarily a social and collective activity in which social groups engage, by telling a mythic narrative in a new way, or applying a new interpretation, or by arranging mythic elements in a novel order to propose a new understanding of an experience. It is in the imaginative space created by these new tellings and interpretations that the possibility of social change becoming a reality can be spoken into being.[22] The mythic system of any social group

19. Lincoln, *Discourse and the Construction of Society,* 3.

20. Ibid., 4–5.

21. Ibid., 7, emphasis added.

22. The speed with which a new myth can be constructed—at least in the political realm—was brought home to me at the time of former U.S. President Ronald Reagan's death. The undergraduates I was teaching at the time had no idea that his presidency had been as conflicted as it was. As persons who had been born near the end of his second term, and whose awareness of political life in the U.S. developed while Reagan was in seclusion because of Alzheimer's disease, they knew him only as the "Great Communicator" who had vanquished the "Evil Empire" of the Soviet Union and made the world "safe" for American "Democracy."

thus serves as a powerful symbol system that can be mobilized either to sustain or transform the society in which it lives. I turn now to explore in more detail how social transformation might take place.

SOCIAL CHANGE, SYMBOL CHANGE, AND THE *HABITUS*

What happens when that which is taken for granted suddenly becomes questionable or questioned? What happens to a society that no longer agrees with its collective "agreements"? Jonathan Z. Smith describes this experience as disjunction, the loss of "fit" or taken-for-grantedness of the complex social arrangements in a given world. [23] At such moments in a society's history, when the world that has been taken for granted suddenly appears to be unfamiliar and chaotic, new meaning structures need to be constructed, or older ones need to be re-signified for that society to survive. Smith has suggested that social change will occur when a society experiences such disjunction, and for better or worse will have to engage in changing or adapting its symbol systems to account for the disjunction.[24] As I have suggested, society's mythic structure is a malleable symbol system that is open to a variety of interpretations and meanings. As such, it not only replicates past social practices and structures, but also can be adjusted (or interpreted in a different way) in order to construct explanations for new ones. For such a change to be completed successfully, a new or revised sustaining mythic structure must be developed and accepted by the society, which allows the *habitus* to resume once again its taken-for-grantedness, although it may have a considerably different look and feel.

In addition to moments of actual crisis and disjunction, Smith describes something he calls "ritualized disjunction."[25] Ritualized disjunction is the way in which a society deals regularly with formative events in its history (especially in its mythical history), by recalling, for example, a time before the community was formed, and the events that led to its creation through struggle and hardship or the trials of its founder. Such ritualized disjunction takes the society through chaos, reversal, and "collective anomie" that is overcome through a structured, patterned process, so that a new world is created, an individual receives a new

23. Smith, "Influence of Symbols on Social Change," 129–46.
24. Ibid., 145.
25. Ibid.

status, or the community is strengthened in some way.[26] Such moments of ritualized disjunction do not threaten the social order; instead, they serve to strengthen and renew it.

If social change *will* happen when a culture or an individual experiences real, not just ritualized disjunction, however, is it possible that social change *can* happen within the ritualized disjunction "event" (ritual), if some members of a social group perceive that there is need for change to occur? Can ritualized disjunction serve as a means to transform the *habitus* in order to avoid social disruption?

I would argue that yes, moments of ritualized disjunction do serve as a moment when it is possible to transform the *habitus*. For example, U.S. presidential campaigns, elections, and inaugurations are moments of ritualized disjunction, when power is transferred from one person to another, and often from one political party to another. This transfer of power and the rituals within which it is embedded are designed to reaffirm the social order, and to create a shared collective agreement that the new president has the power and authority to lead the entire American people.[27] The presidential campaign leading up to the election of the new president and her or his inauguration begins the process, by serving as ritualized disjunction that is designed to allow for the transformation of the *habitus* as candidates seek to persuade voters and the American people in general that their vision for how American society should function is the right one for the next four years. While there is often not much change from one presidency to the next—particularly if there is not a change in party—from time to time there has been a significant renegotiation of what Americans take for granted as the contours of American society. Franklin D. Roosevelt and the "New Deal," and Ronald Reagan's dismantling of it, are examples of when the "taken-for-granted-ness" of American society was transformed through the ritualized disjunction of the U.S. presidential electoral process.

Bourdieu describes such a renegotiation of the *habitus* as subversion—cognitive, political, and heretical—in that someone who is able to

26. Ibid.

27. What was striking in the reception of Barack Obama as President of the United States is the way in which groups in opposition seemed to be seeking to "delegitimize" his Presidency—for example, the "birthers" who tried to say that he was not truly a native born American citizen because he was born in Hawaii rather than on the mainland. It seems to me that this is a dangerous trend in American politics, which may take the electoral process from ritualized to true disjunction.

recognize the need for change must first be able to see that the world as it was is no longer viable (cognitive subversion), and then act on that new vision (political subversion) to create a new social order. The questioning of what has been taken for granted is "heretical" in that it challenges the "orthodox" vision of the world that has been held collectively by the society or group up to that moment. The challenge, for someone seeking to engage in heretical subversion in order to create acceptance for a different topography of the social world, as Bourdieu notes, is how to "sever the adherence to the world of common sense"—in other words, the world as it was "taken for granted"—in order to create a new "common sense"—the social group's acceptance of the new way of being as the way the world is.[28] Simply by suggesting that another way to live together is possible, I would argue, allows for a new common sense to begin to take shape, because such speech makes such a possibility "conceivable and above all credible and thus creat[es] the collective representation and will which contribute to its production."[29]

Re-signifying the mythic system in this way is a critical element for successful social change, especially if such speech uses, in addition to the various symbol systems of the society as its elements, the society's "authorized" language as part of its structure. The use of authorized language links the everyday of the social world with "ultimate" reality and the value system held by the society. Bourdieu has noted that those who can manipulate a social group's symbol system wield power that is as effective as physical or economic power. He describes how critical the use of language is to the manipulation of the symbol system by suggesting that symbolic power is created through the relationship between the one who holds the power and those who submit to that person; that relationship is sustained by using authorized language. In other words, "What creates the power of words and slogans, a power capable of maintaining or subverting the social order, is the belief in the legitimacy of words and of those who utter them."[30]

Persons who can exercise symbolic power are able, through their words, to bring into being what they are speaking about—their words have creative power, in other words. Such persons are able to tap into this power because they have access to the authorized language of the

28. Bourdieu, *Logic of Practice*, 129.
29. Ibid., 127–28.
30. Ibid., 179.

social group.[31] A person duly authorized to speak on a given subject, or in a specific role, or from a particular social position, brings to her or his speaking a host of social relations that imbue the actual spoken words with power beyond their dictionary meanings. That power comes both from the technical expertise of the speaker and her or his authority to speak, which has been granted by a socially recognized, authorized institution that is certified to confer such authority.

Most social groups identify leaders who, by virtue of their leadership positions, are among those who have been "authorized" to speak on behalf of the group. Such persons have the right to "speak" in such a way that their words carry authority with those who hear them—provided, of course, that they are speaking within their duly acknowledged area of expertise, and with those who (must) recognize their authority in the situation in which they speak. Investiture in an authorized role carries "symbolic efficacy" for both parties. Not only do others see that we have authority; we also, by having achieved our position according to the procedures established by the social group, presumably see ourselves in a new light—as someone whose words now carry new weight, new authority to speak on behalf of our organization (within the parameters of our areas of responsibility). The speaking of authorized language carries symbolic power both because others acknowledge it, and because the authorized spokesperson accepts her or his authority to wield such power.[32]

To offer a personal example: I am an ordained elder in the United Methodist Church. When I was ordained, the denomination had a two-stage ordination process in which we were first accepted as ministers "on trial"—probationers—and ordained as deacons with authority to preach and teach, but not to administer the sacraments. After a period of a minimum of two years of supervised service in the pastorate, and formal examinations of the effectiveness of our ministerial practice and the soundness of our theology, we had the opportunity to apply to become full clergy members of the denomination and ordained as elders. The first time I applied, I was not accepted—my practice was superb, but my theology wasn't—but the second time, after learning to describe my theology in more orthodox or "authorized" language (without changing my theology in any way), I was accepted and duly ordained an elder.

31. Bourdieu's concept of "authorized language" is explored in a number of his writings. See, for example, Bourdieu, *Language and Symbolic Power*.

32. Bourdieu, *Language and Symbolic Power*, 119.

The ritual for the ordination of elders in my tradition, once the examinations have been passed, includes a spoken, public examination of the candidates by the bishop before the assembled laypeople, and the laity's spoken affirmation that they will accept the authority of the ordinands in the conduct of their ministry. This public acceptance is followed by a prayer invoking the presence and power of the Holy Spirit, said while the Bishop and other elders lay hands on the head of the ordinand, representing the apostolic succession back to St. Peter as the keeper of the keys of the kingdom (see Matt 16:18–19). The bishop then enjoins the ordinand to "Take thou authority" to fulfill the rights and responsibilities of an elder in the church. The ritual concludes with the giving of a stole, which signifies to the entire world that the wearer has accepted fully the yoke of Christ and will work on behalf of Christ to make real the Kingdom of God in the world. The new elder has one distinctive new responsibility and power, different from deacons and laypersons: the ability to administer the sacraments. The difference in my status as an elder in the church can be seen clearly in the sacrament of Holy Communion; when I speak the "words of institution" over the bread and cup that signify Christ's body and blood, my words—and the actions I perform while saying them—infuse a loaf of bread and (in my tradition) a cup of unfermented grape juice with the real substance of Christ and his saving power. Prior to being ordained an elder, the bread and juice would simply stay bread and juice.

However, as Bourdieu notes, "The symbolic efficacy of words is exercised only in so far as the person subjected to it recognizes the person who exercises it as authorized to do so, or, what amounts to the same thing, only in so far as he fails to realize that, in submitting to it, he himself has contributed, through his recognition, to its establishment."[33] Thus, if I were to speak the same words, and perform the same actions in a Roman Catholic Church for Catholic laypersons, the bread and the wine would presumably not become the body and blood of Christ, because the Catholic Church does not recognize my ordination, and therefore does not acknowledge my speech as authorized to have symbolic efficacy.

Bourdieu further suggests that authorized religious and political language is especially useful in negotiating or renegotiating a disjunction, because such language brings with it "schemes of perception and

33. Ibid., 116.

thought" that can function outside the immediate context in which a society finds itself.[34] The religious and political mythological formations of a given society can thus point both backward in time to moments in a society's history in which a similar crisis situation was handled in a given way, and forward in time to a moment when the society will have passed safely through the crisis and found itself once again in a place of security and safety (although that place may look considerably different from the past). When that place is reached, the *habitus* again resumes its "taken-for-granted-ness," and life for members of the society moves on as though it had never been any different.

Social change can now be conceptualized as the result of a cycle of *habitus* supported by a sustaining myth, which is disrupted by some crisis or other event that challenges the accepted order of things; a process of collective negotiation then takes place to reconfigure and reconstitute the symbol system of the sustaining myth, which then leads to a collectively accepted new version of the *habitus*. Figure 1 is a graphical representation of this process:

FIGURE 1: The Cycle of Social Change

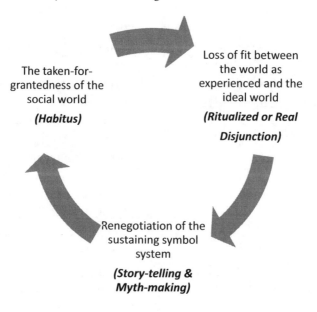

The taken-for-grantedness of the social world
(Habitus)

Loss of fit between the world as experienced and the ideal world
(Ritualized or Real Disjunction)

Renegotiation of the sustaining symbol system
(Story-telling & Myth-making)

---

34. Ibid., 128.

So far, we have seen how the cycle of change works in two different contexts: actual social disjunction and ritualized disjunction. I am suggesting a third way: that it is possible to use this process proactively on behalf of desired or planned social change. If, as Bourdieu suggests, in moments of social crisis—disjunction, to use Smith's term—religious and political language is especially powerful in helping to reconstitute the world, then an intentional use of myth and/or religious and political language should be able to be used at other times to support desired social change. We turn now to explore a theory of the social imagination that may enable us to do just that.

IMAGINATION AND SOCIAL CHANGE

The "always alreadiness" of the world as we experience it is one of the greatest obstacles to social change. We are always born into a world that already exists, and are trained from our earliest moments—without our even being aware of it—to become an unconscious inhabitant of it, to experience it as "natural," as the way the world is. In his article "Imagination in Discourse and In Action," Paul Ricoeur suggests that the always-already nature of society is created by a function of the imagination that links the individual and society, which he describes as intersubjectivity. It is the notion of intersubjectivity that relates me, an individual, to other persons who exist in time, even as I do. Ricoeur proposes that I do not exist as an individual alone in time and space; rather, there are persons who live at the same time as I do, as well as persons who have preceded me in history, and persons who will come after me.[35] We are tied together by a shared "history," which is shaped by traditions passed down from those who came before, and which may be passed on to those who will come after, although, as Ricoeur notes, "This transmission constitutes a tie that can be broken or regenerated."[36] This imaginative intersubjectivity is what helps to create the "always-already" experience of being born into a pre-existing society, while still providing space for new futures to be imagined for and by one's contemporaries and successors, as well as oneself.[37]

Ricoeur's notion of intersubjectivity is thus similar to Bourdieu's notion of the *habitus*. Burton L. Mack has noted that Bourdieu's *habitus*

35. Ricoeur, "Imagination in Discourse and in Action," 179.

36. Ibid.

37. Ibid.

is where a society's "collective agreements reside," and that myth and ritual are the tools used by the members of that society to name, explore, test, challenge, change, and renew those agreements. Mack further notes, "Myths and rituals are designed to exercise the imagination by placing ordinary objects in extraordinary settings and extraordinary figures in ordinary settings."[38] This juxtaposition of objects and settings catches the attention, invites one to note the differences between the mythic experience and one's own, and opens a space in which critical musing on present social arrangements can occur. The result of this reflection either can be a re-negotiation of those arrangements into new forms, or their affirmation and continuance.

As Bourdieu has noted, however, before someone can take on the *habitus*, he or she has to be able to recognize that there is another way to imagine how the world can be.[39] Another way to put it might be, "Changed obedience follows changed imagination."[40] Here is the essence—and the challenge—of social change: before we can change our behavior (obedience), we have to be able to imagine a different way of acting that better embodies our ideal life together. The notion that 'changed obedience follows changed imagination' suggests to me that changed behavior—at both the individual and social levels—is possible, when the individual or social group is able to imagine an alternative course of action. So how, then, does the imagination work?

Often in the Western tradition, the imagination has been set over against "rational" thinking—as though imagination is a less valid way of making sense of the world than logic. More and more, however, imagination is being seen as an equally valid way in which the discrepancies between the way the world is and the way we think it should be are

---

38. Mack, *Christian Myth*, 92.

39. Let me note that I am here taking a position different from most interpreters of Bourdieu by suggesting that it *is* possible for an individual to affect the *habitus*. While on the one hand Bourdieu is clear the *habitus* is the taken-for-grantedness of society that normally is not questioned, I believe his discussion of subversion opens up a space in which it is possible for an individual to effect change, once one sees the "game" for what it is and begins to question it. Bourdieu, *Language and Symbolic Power*, 127–36.

40. Walter Brueggemann suggested that this was a quote by Paul Ricoeur in a lecture as part of Ministers' Convocation, The School of Theology at Claremont, November, 1989. See further Walter Brueggemann, "Restlessness and Greed," 79–110. Although I have not been able to find the exact quotation in any of Ricoeur's writings, he uses the notion of changed imagination in his article, Ricoeur, "Listening to the Parables of Jesus," 239–45.

examined and addressed, and the way in which new possibilities for action in the face of what we experience are generated.[41] By using our imaginations, we are able to tap into resources beyond what we can see, hear, touch, feel, and taste to develop responses to what we experience. We can investigate the experiences of others, imagine what it would be like to have experienced those things ourselves, and decide whether we would have responded in the same or a different way. We can read the myths of our own and other cultures and apply that wisdom to our present situation. We can compare and contrast fictional happenings to our experience, and think about what we would have done if those events had happened to us. We can judge our reactions to certain events by comparing them to the ways in which our neighbors react.

These various understandings of how imagination works are further reinforced by Ricoeur, who suggests that the imagination has the following functions for individuals: 1) it enables individuals to imagine possible courses of action; 2) it enables individuals to test various motivations for choosing to follow an imagined course of action; and 3) it enables individuals to claim their power to act in the imagined way by seeing themselves do what they have imagined.[42] Thus for individuals, imagination helps them first to imagine the possibilities, select between these options by clarifying their motivations for each one, and then claim the power to act by envisioning themselves taking the selected course of action. In all these situations we are exercising "a full range of intellectual operations . . . including what we have traditionally called definition, classification, analysis, theoretical experimentation, judgment, new knowledge, and the formulation of propositions" that are traditionally thought of as the domain of rational, logical thinking—but through the use of our imaginations.[43]

The roles for an individual's imagination described by Ricoeur work equally well for social groups seeking to imagine together alternative possibilities for their collective life. Thus a social group can imagine together possible realignments in their patterns of relating, and clarify as a group what their motivations might be for choosing one possibility over another. They can then claim the power to implement their selected

---

41. See, for example, Byrne, *The Rational Imagination*, and Brueggemann, *The Prophetic Imagination*.

42. Ricoeur, "Imagination in Discourse and In Action," 176–78.

43. Mack, "Gospel and the Gaps," 4.

course of action by working together to develop a plan of action that accounts for the potential obstacles and barriers that may have to be overcome if their alternative is to be put into practice successfully.[44]

In addition, Ricoeur proposes two further ways in which the social imagination works: through ideology and utopia.[45] While acknowledging that both concepts can be problematic and "pathological," Ricoeur also argues that they work dialectically to provide a framework within which society can be both maintained and changed. Ideology performs the function of legitimizing the social status quo, while utopia offers a "nowhere" in which alternative social formations can be imagined that operate in the way in which society "should" function. It is in the tension between what can be imagined and what is currently in place that room for the imagination to play comes into being, and possibilities for social change can occur. We turn now to examine how these "gaps" between ideology and utopia, between actual experience and the ideal, can be utilized on behalf of social change.

A "WORLDLY" THEORY OF THE SOCIAL IMAGINATION

Burton L. Mack has suggested, "Myths are good for creating marvelous narrative worlds in which to stretch the imagination."[46] If persons use their imagination by comparing and contrasting the various "worlds" in which they live, as well as by comparing and contrasting the ideal versions of these worlds to their actual experience, then by identifying and describing these worlds, and seeing how they are used referentially in individual or communal discourses, it should be possible to analyze how persons and communities use them imaginatively to make sense of their daily lives.[47]

44. I will explore such a process in chapter 5.

45. Ricoeur, "Imagination in Discourse and In Action," 181–87.

46. Mack, *The Christian Myth*, 69.

47. The Social Imagination model is adapted from a homiletical theory developed by Burton L. Mack in "Gospel and the Gaps: A Worldly Theory of Preaching," an unpublished manuscript that Prof. Mack generously shared with me while I was working on my Doctor of Ministry dissertation (see Houghtby, "Living Beyond the Horizon," 102–17). I am deeply indebted to the several hundred students who have worked with the model in my World Religions and New Testament courses at The George Washington University; they have helped me clarify the model and its application considerably over the years. Much of Mack's thinking about the mythic imagination addressed in "Gospel and the Gaps" is now in published form in Mack, *Myth and the Christian Nation*.

The Social Imagination theory is built on this premise that persons live within various worlds—worlds such as those of family, religion, culture, society, class, ethnicity, work, profession, etc.—that create a number of frames of references that social groups (and individuals) draw on to make sense of their lives. By identifying specific worlds that may be in play in a given social setting, and then by identifying "authorities" that might link these worlds together, it is possible to "play the gaps" among the worlds to reflect on the differences among the variety of worlds themselves, and between the worlds as idealized and experienced. This reflection can then lead to adjustments and new social agreements by which the group both constructs and maintains its shared social setting. Seeing this adjudication process in action can help an observer understand the contours of a world that may be different from her or his own, because of culture or historical distance. It can also help that observer to understand her or his own world better, by contrasting it to the social group under observation.

Four Worlds of the Social Imagination

To show the social imagination in action, the theory becomes a model for application by first selecting the worlds and authorities that reasonably can be assumed to shape the topography of the social group's imagination that is under consideration.[48] While one might be quite specific (developing the model for a specific agency within the U.S. federal government, for example), for our purposes we will construct a general model that can then be applied to a variety of social groups. For ease of description, we will call the social group a "community," which implies that these are not simply discrete individuals who happen to be in the same place at the same time; rather they are individuals who join together intentionally with some sense of mutual relationship and shared purpose (although how each person defines that purpose may differ somewhat), and even though they may be scattered geographically and across time. Out of the various worlds available to us, there are four that seem particularly useful in constructing a general model of the so-

---

48. Mack's theory was developed for an explicitly Christian social setting. I am generalizing the theory so that it is applicable in any social setting. For example, in addition to using the model in religion classes, I also use it as a tool for organizational change in leadership courses for government managers and executives in local and federal government settings.

cial imagination: the Communal World, the Society World, the Culture World, and the Mythic World.

The Communal World

We begin with the Communal World of life and practice for the social group under investigation. This world represents the way in which the community functions in the present, although it most likely has some sense of continuity with previous generations, which may well be an imaginative link. While it may look considerably different from the community described by the mythic world (see below), it is understood to be anchored in, and coterminous with, that world.

The Communal World is shaped by the community's belief system, the way it lives its life together, and may well include a "language" that is unique to its self-understanding, as well as unique architecture that helps to shape the community's living space. Among the features of the Communal World that may set it apart from other groups in society include: how it defines the duties and responsibilities of its members, its procedures for accepting new members, identifying and confirming leadership, and making decisions as a group, as well as how it marks the passage of persons who leave the community. The Communal World is also shaped by how the mythic world is referred to and used in the community's life, the community's process for dealing with persons in the larger society who are not members of the community itself, and how the community relates to the surrounding culture within which it is embedded.[49]

The Society World

The second world of our model is hinted at in the above description: the larger Society World within which the community functions. For all intents and purposes, the Society World is the "real" world in which persons live, a world shaped by institutions such as the family, work, religions, and the role of government in everyday life, as well as patterns of activity such as the society's economic and justice systems. It is the world in which people behave as we expect them to behave, in which our insti-

49. Let me note that this description of the Communal World presumes that there are sub-groups within a larger "society." In some situations—such as a small tribe in the Amazonian rain forest—it might be difficult to identify much, if any, distinction between the Communal world and the Society world. In such a hypothetical situation, individual family units might provide a basis for analysis.

tutions work without our having to think about it, and in which we know how others will expect us to behave. It is also the world within which the Communal World is embedded, although the community may have different expectations of its members (e.g., no drinking or dancing) than persons in the Society World who are not members of the community.

THE CULTURE WORLD

The third world of our model is the Culture World, which comprises all the ways in which a given people "bends nature to [its] will."[50] Among these activities are: language, art, values, ideals, ideologies, notions of what is "right" and what is "wrong," what constitutes good taste, civility, and proper gender roles, as well as more tangible things such as the plan of cities and how houses and furniture are designed and used. These activities combine in the culture world to create a system of symbols that encompass the deepest held values and beliefs of a given society. Religious traditions both help to produce and are produced by the Culture World. For example, a dominant religious tradition may shape and influence the Culture World in a significant way—e.g., the use of the Golden Rule as an ethical standard for persons in the U.S., even if they are not Christian and have no idea that it is recorded in the Gospel of Matthew, or that the same concept can be found in a variety of religious traditions. Not too surprisingly, the Culture and Society Worlds are closely aligned, as are the Mythic World and the Communal World of life and practice.

THE MYTHIC WORLD

The final world for our model is that of the Mythic World, which is constituted by the community's idealized and epic past and/or future. This world may be populated by gods and goddesses, as well as by ancestors and founding figures of the community. It includes "memories" of how the community was started, where it came from, challenges it overcame and successes it achieved. To some extent, it has a "once upon a time" feel to it, but it is also likely to be understood as being in some sense "historical" for the community. Furthermore, it may also include some hoped for future state, in which, for example, the righteous are blessed and the wicked are punished, or God (or God's emissary) returns to usher in a new creation.

---

50. Berger, *Sacred Canopy*, 6.

There is clearly some overlap among the worlds—e.g., the role of the mythic past in shaping a community's understanding of its present life and practice, or the impact of far-flung suburban space (the culture world) on decisions about gasoline taxes (the society world). It is also clear that there are gaps between the worlds. A Christian community, for example, hearing about Jesus' visit with the Samaritan Woman in its Sunday morning worship service, will experience a gap between what the details of the story may have meant to the gospel's first hearers and how the community understands the story in the twenty-first century. Some questions the gap might pose: why are the disciples surprised to find Jesus speaking with the Woman? What is significant about her identification as a Samaritan? Is it odd that she has come to the well alone at midday? And so on. In another example, the ongoing debate in the United States about what constitutes marriage and who can enter into it illuminates a gap between our cultural assumptions and changing social patterns of behavior. Many other examples could be given of such gaps. How then might we bridge these gaps between worlds, as well as acknowledge the overlaps among them, in order to see a community's imagination at work?

Four Authorities of the Social Imagination

As a way to connect the four worlds, Mack proposed the use of "authorities" that could be understood as "an autonomous source from which instructive data can be taken and combined" in the process of exploring how connections are made and gaps are bridged.[51] The four authorities in the Social Imagination model are: foundational texts, which connect the culture and mythic worlds; tradition, which connects the mythic and communal worlds; experience, which connects the communal and society worlds; and reason, which connects the society and culture worlds. The four authorities can serve as tools to help bridge the gaps between the various worlds, as well as help to shape the features of the worlds, as we shall see below.

FOUNDATIONAL TEXTS

The first authority is that of foundational texts such as sacred scriptures, national constitutions, and other charter documents for the community

---

51. Mack, "The Gospel and the Gaps," 53.

under examination. The documents themselves, as artifacts that can be read and referred to as physical things, both establish the ideals imagined in the Mythic World, and supply many of the values and norms that create the Culture World. The authority of the texts as tangible things in themselves thus serves as a bridge between these two worlds. The influence of moral norms in Western culture such as the Ten Commandments, because of a common scriptural text, is an example of that bridging.

TRADITION

The second authority is that of tradition. This authority connects the Mythic World to the Communal World of the social group's life and practice, and helps to make the ideals of the Mythic World real in the lives of the members of that community. Tradition includes customs, communal laws, regulations, processes, procedures, and precedence that seek to "operationalize" the ideals of the Mythic World in the community's present life and practice. It also includes the history of interpretation of those processes and conventions over time. In addition, it includes the ways in which the mythic stories and traditions have been used to support the values and ethical orientation of the community's life together. For example, the recent debate about whether the Ten Commandments can be displayed in U.S. courtrooms is an example of how the United States renegotiates its tradition; for many decades its (Christian) citizens took for granted that the Decalogue is foundational to the U.S. system of laws and standards of ethical behavior. The debate centered around whether the Ten Commandments are a passage from two religions' sacred scriptures, and thereby prohibited in public spaces through the constitutional principle of the separation of church and state, or whether they have achieved an authoritative status outside of their religious context by informing the country's legal institutions historically, thereby making it appropriate for them to be displayed in the public space of U.S. courthouses—the symbolic guarantor of this constitutional principle.

EXPERIENCE

The third authority is that of experience, which connects the Communal World of life and practice to the Society World, as persons function both as members of the community and as members of the surrounding society. This authority bridges the gap between how the community imagines itself as distinct from the larger social world in which it is embedded, and the requirements and expectations that the larger society places on all its citizens. The example of public school students in various European countries who want to be allowed to wear symbols of their religion to class (primarily young Muslim women wearing headscarves), offers an example of this gap.[52]

REASON

The fourth authority is reason, which connects the Culture and Society Worlds. Reason, part of the West's legacy from the Enlightenment,[53] suggests that we make judgments about the reasonableness of our cultural values held up against our social experience. It also suggests that we use deliberation and argumentation to persuade one another that our ideas about how the world works—or should work—make sense. Based on these reflections we make together, we adjust the contours of either our Culture World or our Society World when we face incongruity between the two worlds. For example, roles for women in U.S. society have changed dramatically in the past fifty years, and cultural values have had to be examined and rethought in light of the new patterns of activity engaged in by women. The culture clash between so-called "family values" and the actual structure of the family in our society is another example of incongruity between the Culture and Society Worlds; the increasing acceptance of "non-traditional" families can be seen as an example of the use of reason in adjudicating the tensions that result from this gap.

The Social Imagination Model

Our model is now complete, with four worlds connected by four authorities. By connecting them in this way, the model creates an arena within which it is possible to see a given community's imagination at work. It also creates an arena within which a social group may seek to exercise its imagination in order to address an issue of concern to itself. Discourse in such an arena takes advantage of the ideas, experiences, values, actions, histories, biographies, and other data that are a part ei-

---

52. For a representative discussion of this issue, see Ward, "Shabina Begum and the Headscarf Girls," 119–31.

53. It should be noted that earlier cultures also have an understanding of "reason"; *logos* as the rational, life-giving and organizing principle of the cosmos is a concept from Greek philosophy that shapes much of the New Testament. I will be looking at rhetoric as a tool of reason in my analysis of the biblical passage I explore in subsequent chapters.

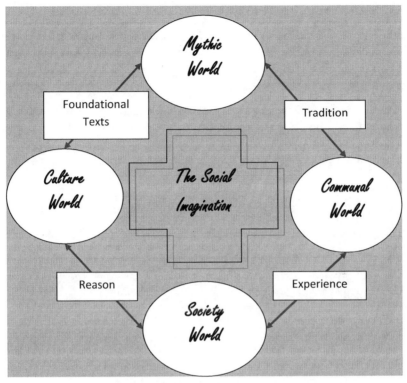

FIGURE 2: The Social Imagination Model

ther of the worlds or the connecting authorities, in order to think about the situation at hand and develop a response to it. Questions that might be asked in the arena include: Has this situation ever happened before? If so, how did persons respond then? Is there someone who came up with a totally new response to some other situation? If so, what happened? Is there anything from that experience we could apply here? What values are at stake in this situation? How can we stay true to those that are important to us? Are there other values we should emphasize? And so on. A caveat is in order here, however. While the above description of the model and its graphical depiction shown above creates an ordered picture of the connections and relationships between the worlds and the authorities, the imaginative process is much messier; the authorities may actually be used to link different worlds from those proposed above, while the worlds themselves may overlap and gap in various ways. For the purposes of this discussion, however, we will let the model stand in an ordered way.

Guidelines for Applying the Social Imagination Model

We turn in the next chapter to apply the Social Imagination model to an ancient text, to see if we can discern how a community in the past might have used the elements that comprise the model to think about how to construct new social arrangements for itself at a time of social change. To do so, it may be useful to have some guidelines in mind as a way to help follow the analysis. In his original discussion of the model, Burton Mack identified several guidelines that would be helpful in creating a conversation on some topic of interest to a social group.[54] These guidelines are:

1. Touch on two or three of the worlds intentionally;

2. Make connections between the worlds by paying attention to how they are ranked, compared, etc.

3. Acknowledge honestly the incongruity between the worlds as imagined and the worlds as experienced;

4. Stay within the frame of reference provided by the biblical texts, the political tradition, and the cultural or social points being addressed;

5. Play the gaps with a constructive proposal in mind.

In order to use the model analytically, I have adapted the guidelines in the following way:

1. Identify which worlds may be in play.

2. See how the worlds are ranked or compared—does one world take precedence over another? (e.g., is the world of present experience compared negatively to the "good old days" when life was less complicated?)

3. Identify the incongruity between the worlds that is being addressed. Is the incongruity between one world and another, or is it between a world as imagined and that world as experienced by members of the community?

4. Identify how the authorities are used to bridge, explain, collapse, or otherwise make sense of the incongruity.

5. How does the author "play the gaps" to make a constructive proposal?

54. Mack, "Gospel and the Gaps," 112–13.

In chapter 5, I will summarize my findings by looking at all five of the guidelines, to see how Luke and his audience might have understood the information I have gathered, before moving to a discussion of how a contemporary social group might apply these findings to their own situation. To give the reader a road map for the next three chapters, however, it may be useful to see how I will be developing the first guideline throughout those chapters.

GUIDELINE 1: IDENTIFY WHICH WORLDS MAY BE IN PLAY

In the case of the Bent-Over-Woman story, my contention is that all four worlds of the model are visible in the way in which Luke crafts his narrative. Here are the key elements from each world that will be addressed in my discussion:

- Mythic World (Chapter 2)
  - Sabbath observance
  - Promises to David/Abraham
  - Exodus traditions/release from bondage
  - Sabbatical/Jubilee Years
  - Isaiah's Vision of the Restoration of Israel
- Society World (Chapter 3)
  - Physical condition
  - Slavery—real and metaphoric
  - Gender roles and expectations
  - Power in relationships (e.g., social status)
- Communal World (Chapter 4)
  - We are transformed from our prior condition to a new one.
    - Jesus is the "Lord" who has set us free from our slave status and
    - Jesus as the Lord has restored us to our twin inheritances as children of Abraham and David's descendents.
  - We're all in it together, regardless of social status, physical condition, gender, or ethnicity.
    - We can live together as a "discipleship of equals."[55]

55. Schüssler Fiorenza, "Jesus and the Politics of Interpretation," 354.

- Culture World (Chapters 2, 3, and 4)
  - We make sense of our world using cultural tools available to us:
    - Literary genres (e.g., διήγησις,[56] Romance novels)
    - Rhetorical stratagems (e.g., elaborated *chreia*, midrash)
  - Meaning of disability, gender, liberation

Now, with our roadmap in hand, let us head off on our journey of discovery as we examine how Luke has used his social imagination to write a narrative that continues to compel readers today.

---

56. *Diēgēsis* (διήγησις) is a narrative genre in Greco-Roman literature which Theon describes as "language descriptive of things that have happened or as though they had happened." He goes on to state that there are six elements included in διήγησις: "the person, whether that be one or many; and the action done by the person; and the place where the action was done; and the time at which it was done; and the manner of the action; and sixth, the cause of these things. Since these are the most comprehensive elements from which it is composed, a complete narration (διήγησις) consists of all of them and of things related to them and one lacking any of these is deficient." Theon, "On Narrative," in Kennedy, *Progymnasmata*, 28. Luke indicates that in writing his "orderly account" he follows in the footsteps of those who have compiled a narrative (διήγησις) before him "of the things that have been accomplished among us" (Luke 1:1–4).

2

Daughter of Abraham Established Forever

The Mythic and Culture Worlds of the Bent-Over Woman

INTRODUCTION

WITH THIS CHAPTER, I begin the application of the Social Imagination model. My object of study is a short passage from the
Gospel of Luke, the story of the Bent-Over Woman (Luke 13:10–17). My
argument will be that this short pericope—a mere 8 verses—provides
an important interpretive clue for understanding Luke's social vision for
his audience, a vision laid out over the course of the Gospel and the
Acts of the Apostles. I will also suggest that, in creating this vision, Luke
was imagining an alternative future for his audience, a future in which
participation in the life of the community that gathered in Jesus' name
was open to all persons, regardless of gender, social status, ethnicity, or
physical condition.

In this chapter, I apply the lens of the Mythic World to the
story of the Bent-Over Woman. In chapter 3, I will apply the lens
of the Society World. In chapter 4, I conclude my analysis by looking through the lens of the Communal World. Since culture contains
society and is shaped by myth, the Culture World of the model serves
as a connector for my analysis in each chapter, along with the four
authorities of the model: foundational texts, tradition, experience,
and reason. In each chapter, I will identify key "topographical" features of the worlds as Luke seems to emphasize them, in order to see
Luke's imagination at work more clearly.[1]

1. I am using male pronouns and the name "Luke" to refer to the author of the third
gospel in the New Testament for convenience, without conjecturing about whom the
author may have been. I follow the same convention for the other canonical gospels.

Before turning to my in-depth analysis of the pericope, let me note that all four canonical gospels have a story about an unnamed woman that seems to be used by the author to suggest something about the role of Jesus and the composition of the people who make up the community that follows him. In Mark, the story is about a Syro-Phoenician Woman (Mark 7:24–30), whose insistence that Jesus is *her* messiah, too, expands Jesus' understanding about his role as Messiah. Through this interaction, Jesus is shown discovering that his messiahship extends beyond the boundaries of Israel to include all those who believe in him, regardless of their ethnic background.

Matthew uses this story from his Markan source in approximately the same way, although he will describe the woman's identity as Canaanite, rather than Syro-Phoenician, focusing on the religious implications of her interaction with Jesus (Matt 15:21–28). It will be the Woman's faith in Jesus' role and power that serves as the standard by which persons can claim membership in the community that follows him. Even the Gospel of John uses this device, although the interaction comes somewhat earlier in the plotline of Jesus' ministry for its author. In his interaction with the Samaritan Woman (John 4:4–42), John's Jesus first reveals that he is, indeed, the messiah for whom both her people and his people have been looking—and that those who worship God "in spirit and in truth," regardless of their origins—will be a part of the community of Jesus' followers.

Luke, however, has no need to convince his audience that non-Jews are acceptable for membership, if, in fact, the scholarly consensus is true that he is writing for a mixed—or even primarily—Gentile audience.[2] Just as he took the anointing story from his Markan source and completely reworked it in order to better fit his mythmaking purposes (in the process making it almost unrecognizable as the same story),[3] so I think Luke utilizes the *function* of the Syro-Phoenician Woman story in

---

I am in agreement with the scholarly consensus that the same author wrote both the gospel known as Luke and the Acts of the Apostles that is also included in the New Testament canon.

2. The tradition that the author of the third gospel was writing for a Gentile audience goes back to the second century CE. See, for example, Eusebius's discussion of Luke as the companion of Paul (3.4) and his citation of Irenaeus (5.8) in Eusebius, *History of the Church*, 67, 154 respectively.

3. See Corley, "The Anointing of Jesus in the Synoptic Tradition," 61–72, for a discussion of the two-story vs. one-story proposal in the scholarly literature.

his Markan source by replacing Mark's story with one he writes himself. Apparently, this story is better suited to helping his audience understand Jesus' role as Luke conceptualizes it, as well as how he visualizes the nature of the social group that follows this Jesus.

Since, therefore, all four of our canonical gospel authors have used such a story for such a purpose, it appears that for first century Christian writers, to paraphrase Claude Levi-Strauss loosely, "women are good to think with."[4] How, then, is Luke "thinking with" this woman? What role does she play in his stated goal of setting out "an orderly account" for his reader, so that he (or she) may know "the truth" about these events (Luke 1:1–4)? Let us turn now to explore this story in more detail.

THE TEXT AS TEXT:
FORM AND STRUCTURE OF LUKE 13:10–17

The story of the Bent-Over Woman is found only in Luke 13:10–17, so it does not come directly from his Markan source or the Q material, suggesting it has been composed by the author himself. Because it is found only in Luke, it has not received as much scholarly attention as pericopae with parallel passages in Mark and Matthew.[5] Moreover, it has received little attention in church or academic circles, perhaps since it is a story in which Jesus tells no parable. However, because it is part of the material that Luke alone contains, clearly the author felt it was a story that was important to achieving his goal of presenting "an orderly account" so that his addressee Theophilus "might know the truth concerning the things of which you have been informed" (Luke 1:3–4). Here is my own translation of the story of the Bent-Over Woman:

---

4. This seems to be true for Jewish authors as well; Philo, for example, will use named women in his writings to allegorize various qualities of Israel. See, e.g., *De Congressu Quaerendae Eruditionis Gratia*. There is also a long tradition in Greek philosophy of using women to think through issues about society; cf. Aristotle, *On Politics*, Plato, *The Republic*, Xenophon, *Oeconomicus*, and Aristophanes, *Ecclesiazusai (Assembly-Women)*.

5. I also suspect that Rudolf Bultmann's dismissal of it as the most poorly written of the Sabbath controversy stories had something to do with the pericope's invisibility to scholars. See Bultmann, *History*, 12–13. See also Hamm, "Freeing," 23–44, and n.2. I am indebted to Hamm's article for many of my observations about the text, although I will propose some additional—and in some cases, different—ideas about Luke's intention in the story.

Luke 13:10 And he was teaching in one of the synagogues on the Sabbath. 11And behold, a woman having a spirit of weakness for eighteen years [appeared]; she was bent over and was without the ability to raise up herself fully. 12 But seeing her, Jesus called her to him and said, "Woman, you have been set free from your weakness," 13 and he laid his hands on her and immediately she was raised up, and she was praising God. 14 But the head of the synagogue, responding to [Jesus' words and action], angry because Jesus healed on the Sabbath, was saying to the crowd, "There are six days in which work must be done; come therefore on those days for your healing, and not the day of the Sabbath."

15 Answering him, therefore, the Lord said, "You pretenders! Doesn't every one of you on the Sabbath unloose your ox and donkey from the manger and lead it away to drink? 16 And this woman, being a daughter of Abraham, whom Satan was binding for lo! these eighteen years—ought not she [also] be set free from these bindings on the day of the Sabbath?"

17 At these sayings of his, all his opponents were ashamed, and the crowd was rejoicing at all the memorable things performed by him.

At first glance, it seems possible that the pericope could fit into any or all of three standard genres in the gospels: miracle stories, exorcisms, and Sabbath controversy/healing stories. But there are several clues to indicate that it does not fit into the typical pattern for any of these genres, which suggests that Luke, an adept writer of Greek among the gospel authors,[6] is trying to communicate something different by telling the story in this particular way. As Joel B. Green has observed about this story in relationship to the miracle story genre, "One is immediately impressed with how this pericope departs from the normal form of a miracle story, and, in fact, from all normal form categories."[7] He notes that while Luke regularly adds a concluding stage of impression/response to the three-part miracle story form of exposition/history, technique, and success/proof (v. 17), even that typical Lukan pattern is changed by the addition of the dialogue between the synagogue ruler and Jesus in vv. 14–16.[8]

Another hint that Luke's authorial intention is different in this story is that it differs considerably from other Lukan exorcisms. Typically in

6. Aune, *The New Testament in Its Literary Environment*, 116.

7. Green, "Jesus and a Daughter of Abraham," 644.

8. Ibid.

Luke, Jesus speaks to the spirit possessing the individual, and the spirit is either "rebuked" (ἐπιτιμάω) or "cast out" (ἐκβάλλω), resulting in the spirit leaving the afflicted person. But here, Luke uses a form of the Greek verb ἀπολύω, meaning "to set free."[9] It is the only time in the context of an exorcism or a healing story in the entire gospel corpus that Jesus tells the victim that she (or he) has been "set free" from her (or his) ailment.[10]

But this passage not only differs from other gospel exorcisms, it is also inconsistent with the typical Sabbath controversy genre of the gospels. Clearly, this *is* a Sabbath controversy story, for Jesus is unmistakably portrayed as being in conflict with a synagogue leader on the Sabbath; the surface layer of the story is therefore about the appropriate way to observe the fourth commandment. As is standard in this genre, Jesus' interpretation of the commandment conflicts with the authority's interpretation. However, Luke has not followed the typical pattern for stories in the genre; in order to account for this, Bultmann, in his *History of the Synoptic Tradition*, proposed that it was a clumsy adaptation of Mark 3:1–6, the Sabbath controversy/healing story about a man with a withered hand—even though that story is paralleled directly in Luke 6:6–11.[11] The problem for Bultmann was that in the story of the Bent-Over Woman, the "healing" precedes the discussion between Jesus and the authorities, a fact which he concludes "renders impossible any organic connection of the story with its conclusion."[12]

9. Luke uses the perfect passive form, indicating that the event was accomplished in the past, with results existing in the present. Hamm suggests that surely this is a use of the "divine" passive (Hamm, "Freeing," 29). Luke's use of the perfect passive in this passage parallels his use of the same verb form when Jesus announces that the sins of the woman who anoints him have been forgiven in Luke 7:48.

10. Luke does use a form of ἀπολύω in the story of the man healed of dropsy in Luke 14:1–6. However, he does not use it to describe how the person's illness is transformed, as happens with the Bent-Over Woman. Jesus is described as "taking hold" (ἐπιλαβόμενος) of the man, healing him (ἰάσατο), and then releasing him (ἀπέλυσεν) after the healing is performed. It is also interesting to note that the demons that afflicted Mary Magdalene "came out" of her (Luke 8:2b); even she was not "set free," while the women mentioned with her were healed (τεθεραπευμέναι) from their infirmities (ἀσθενειῶν), Luke 8:2a). In Acts 16, when Paul meets a slave girl with a spirit of divination, he speaks to the spirit rather than the woman, just as Jesus does in the other Lukan exorcisms.

11. Bultmann, *History,* 12–13. See also the discussion in Hamm, "Freeing," n. 2.

12. Bultmann, *History,* 12. Hamm also disagrees with Bultmann, seeing a coherently written narrative with setting, introduction of the woman, action of Jesus in response to seeing the woman, responses to Jesus' action by the woman and the synagogue leader,

However, the juxtaposition of the narrative of the healing followed by the discussion between Jesus and the synagogue leader does follow the pattern for an elaborated *chreia*. A *chreia* is a short anecdote or story that often concluded with an unexpected response on the part of the main character, who was usually a well-known figure. The story was then elaborated in various ways, and served as the basic school exercise for persons learning the art of rhetoric.[13] It is this rhetorical device that Luke has selected in order to persuade his audience that what he is arguing in the story is important for the community to hear and understand.

In the gospels, pronouncement stories and controversy stories often seem to follow the pattern for elaborated *chreiai*, with characteristics similar to Cynic *chreiai* in the Greek philosophical tradition, in that they are often used to depict Jesus playing off conventional social beliefs and practices in order to establish a different frame of reference or interpretation.[14] *Chreiai* could address sayings, actions, or be "mixed"— anecdotes recording a combined saying and action that took place at the same time.[15] In the case of the Bent-Over Woman, Jesus both announces that the woman has been set free *and* lays his hands on her, at which point she is able to stand up straight, suggesting a mixed *chreia*. The elaboration pattern is as follows:[16]

Jesus' response to the leader, and two responses to Jesus' word—one negative (the adversaries) and one positive (the crowd). Hamm, "Freeing," 25–26.

13 For information on the elaboration of *chreiai* see Mack, *Rhetoric and the New Testament*. See also Mack's detailed discussion of the elaboration pattern as a school exercise in "Elaboration of the *Chreia* in the Hellenistic School," in Mack and Robbins, *Patterns of Persuasion*, 31–67, and Mack's exploration of the pattern in Philo in two essays, "Decoding the Scriptures," 81–115, and "Argumentation in Philo's *De Sacrificiis*," 1–32.

14. Mack, "Elaboration of the *Chreia*," 50, 65–67.

15. Kennedy, *Progymnasmata*, 15.

16. I am using my own translation here.

TABLE 1: Elaboration Pattern of Luke 13:10–17

Elaboration Pattern Component	Scripture Verses
Narrative: *Healing on the Sabbath (v.10–13)*	10 And he was teaching in one of the synagogues on the Sabbath. 11And behold, a woman having a spirit of weakness for eighteen years [appeared]; she was bent over and was without the ability to raise up herself fully. 12 But seeing her, Jesus called her to him and said, "Woman, you have been set free from your weakness," 13 and he laid his hands on her and immediately she was raised up, and she was praising God.
Objection/issue: *One ought not to work (heal) on the Sabbath (v.14)*	14 But the head of the synagogue, responding to [Jesus' words and action], angry because Jesus healed on the Sabbath, was saying to the crowd, "There are six days in which work must be done; come therefore on those days for your healing, and not the day of the Sabbath.
Argument /rebuttal (comprised of the next four components): *One is obligated to release those in bondage on the Sabbath*	
Citation: Scriptural commandment (Deut 5:12–15) giving the rationale for Sabbath rest that the Exodus meant freedom from bondage for the entire household, including the "ox and donkey" (v. 15ab)	15 Answering him, therefore, the Lord said, "You pretenders! Doesn't every one of you on the Sabbath unloose ...
Analogy: ox and donkey (v. 15b)	... your ox and donkey from the manger and lead it away to drink?
Example: (less than to more than) so also the woman/daughter of Abraham (v.16a)	16 And this woman, being a daughter of Abraham, whom Satan was binding for lo! these eighteen years—
Maxim (implied): The Sabbath is for Freedom! (v. 16b)	ought not she [also] be set free from these bindings on the day of the Sabbath?"
Conclusion (encomium): *The Sabbath must be liberating for all (v. 17)*	17 At these sayings of his, all his opponents were ashamed, and the crowd was rejoicing at all the memorable things performed by him.

The narrative section (Luke 13:10–13) sets the stage by describing Jesus' interaction with the woman. A challenge is then issued by the synagogue leader that the Sabbath is not a day on which healing should take place (Objection, v. 14). It is in the verbs that the controversy is played out, and is centered on what one is obligated (δεῖ) to do on the Sabbath.[17] The synagogue leader argues that there are six days on which it is necessary (δεῖ) to do work (ἐργάζομαι), but those days do not include the Sabbath; to heal (θεραπεύω) is work, and therefore should not take place on the Sabbath. Jesus, on the other hand, in describing the woman's condition as bondage rather than disease, and explicitly citing the Deuteronomic rationale for observing the Sabbath (Israel's freedom from bondage in Egypt) by naming the ox and donkey as among those who should rest on the Sabbath, argues that it is necessary (δεῖ) that the woman be set free precisely *because* it is the Sabbath.[18]

In his response to the synagogue leader, Luke's Jesus uses the rhetorical argument "from the lesser to the greater" (*a minori ad maius*). This pattern encourages agreement with the speaker's objective by allowing his/her hearers to agree with a smaller, generally less controversial point first. Then, having agreed with that point, the audience should find themselves agreeing with the main argument by analogy. Jesus' response to the synagogue leader thus reminds his listeners who is obligated by the commandment to keep Sabbath rest: "you, your son or your daughter, your male or female slave, your ox or your donkey, or any of your livestock, or the resident alien in your towns, so that your male and female slave may rest as well as you" (Deut 5:14). By starting with what is low on the list—the livestock—and asking his hearers to agree that the commandment does, in fact, demand the liberation of the ox and donkey, Jesus then is able to secure their agreement on what is higher on the list, the daughter.[19] In specifically naming the ox and donkey as the

---

17. Fitzmyer, *Luke X–XX*, 1013–14. See also Hamm, "Freeing," 33.

18. Burton Mack notes that "in the Greek tradition of the progymnasmata the terms for work and elaboration (πόνος; ἐργάζεσθαι) were stock terms for playing with the analogies between practice and thinking" (personal communication with the author, 12/06/2008). The use of ἐργάζομαι as a key element of the argumentation suggests that Luke is inviting his audience to review the consistency between their own practice and beliefs, especially around liberation issues that may be at stake in the group.

19. "Daughter" is an element of two other healing stories in the gospels: the entwined stories of Jairus' Daughter and the Woman with a Hemorrhage, to whom Jesus says, "Daughter, your faith has made you well" (Luke 8:48//Mark 5:34//Matt 9:22).

lesser part of the analogy, Luke is citing the Deuteronomic version of the commandment. There is also a version of the commandment in Exodus 20:8–11, which does not specify particular kinds of livestock, only the category of livestock generally.[20] Luke thus clearly expects his audience to focus on Deuteronomy's rationale for keeping the Sabbath: liberation from bondage.[21]

With this overview of the form and rhetorical structure of the pericope in place, I turn now to explore how Luke appears to be working in this passage with his social group's foundational texts, the mythic world those texts describe for him, and his use of the tradition of reinterpreting those texts to address changing social and historical contexts within the life of his community.

––––––––––––––––

In chapter 3, I will explore the social role and status of daughters in more detail, especially in relationship to the Exodus 21 passage dealing with daughters sold into debt slavery. Furthermore, the description of the Woman as "daughter of Abraham," links this story to the story of Zacchaeus in 19:1–10, who is identified as "son of Abraham." Zacchaeus' actions are linked to the provisions for restitution prescribed by the guilt offering legislation in Lev 6:1–7, which I believe then also links the Zacchaeus story to the anointing story. I will discuss this connection in more detail below. Both the Bent-Over Woman and Zacchaeus embody John the Baptist's claim that God will raise up other children of Abraham if the present generation does not repent (Luke 3:8).

20. Hamm argues that the Exodus version is also in mind, given Luke's usage of ἐνδόξοις (marvels/memorable acts) in the final verse of the pericope. Used in the Torah (Deut 10:21 and Exod 34:10), "the *endoxa* are the Lord's works during the conquest of the land—i.e., the prelude to the rest which the Sabbath commemorates, along with the divine rest after creation" (Hamm, "Freeing," 27). I don't disagree that Luke would assume that both rationales would be in his audience's mind when they heard the story (in fact, I think he counts on it), only that his emphasis is on the Deuteronomic rationale.

21. A striking feature of the narrative is the way in which the two men treat the woman. As noted above, Jesus informs the Woman *directly* that she "has been set free" from her infirmity, while the synagogue leader—by way of his comments to the crowd—chastises the woman *indirectly* (and Jesus obliquely) for violating the Sabbath commandment by coming to "be cured" on the Sabbath. Of course, as far as we know the woman has *not* come on the Sabbath to be cured—she is simply there in the gathering according to the text; it is *Jesus* who notices her and calls her over to where he is teaching. It is interesting to note that Luke uses the same verb to describe Jesus' calling of the disciples to him in Luke 6:13, prior to his naming of the twelve. I will discuss the implications of this word choice in more detail in chapter 4.

THE SOCIAL IMAGINATION MODEL:
LUKE'S MYTHIC WORLD

As the reader will recall from the previous chapter, the Mythic World is the world that holds the community's idealized past, including memories of how the community was begun, the role of key founding figures, including deities, and significant events that have shaped the way in which the community lives. The Mythic World has two connecting authorities: foundational texts and tradition. Foundational texts are those texts that a community holds sacred or thinks of as source documents for its life and practice, such as national constitutions or charters, scriptures, etc. The authority of tradition is formed by the way in which ideals of the Mythic World are "operationalized" in the present life of the community, as well as the history of interpretation of those ideals from the past to the present.

For Luke, the mythic world that is most clearly in view in the Bent-Over Woman pericope and throughout the gospel is the Jewish mythic world. However, for Luke it is a mythic world that appears to be in need of redescription,[22] as Jesus is depicted constantly as revising "official" interpretations of its laws and practices. To engage in his project of redescription, Luke cleverly "plays the gaps" between what are depicted as standard Jewish interpretations of religious, social, and cultural practices, and how Jesus, as the one who "teaches with authority" (Luke 4:36), reinterprets these practices for Jesus' followers, whom he seems to suggest are the true Israel, the true beneficiaries of the promises given to Abraham.[23] What I will be seeking to uncover through my analysis are the elements of his audience's mythic world that Luke is drawing upon

---

22. I use the term "redescription" in the sense given to it by Burton L. Mack as he summarizes the fourfold methodological approach of Jonathan Z. Smith to studying religion in Mack, "On Redescribing Christian Origins," 256–59. I realize this is an anachronistic application of Smith's method, since the author of Luke would not have been privy to Smith's categories of analysis (description, comparison, redescription, rectification). However, as I show in this study, the author of Luke is clearly engaging in a similar thought process as he presents his story of the life of Jesus and the earliest followers of Jesus, in contradistinction to other Jewish and Christian interpretations of what it means to be, not just followers of Jesus, but also heirs of the promises to Abraham, to Israel, and to David.

23. David Aune notes that Sabbath observance was one of the traditional markers of Jewish social and religious identity (Aune, *The New Testament in Its Literary Environment*, 137); Luke's addition of this story to his gospel suggests that community identity issues are being negotiated in this passage.

in order to establish an alternative imagined epic "history" that better authorizes the social interests and patterns of relating with which his group seems to be experimenting.[24]

While he argues for his vision using Greco-Roman literary techniques throughout his gospel, the author of Luke seems to reflect imaginatively on the traditions that are available to him in the mythic world shared by himself and his audience by using the Jewish practice of midrash. Midrash uses ancient authoritative traditions to reflect upon contemporary issues of importance to a given community.[25] There are several traditions from the scriptures that Luke draws upon to deepen the meaning of his story of the Bent-Over Woman and enhance its interpretative value for the entire narrative he is telling in Luke-Acts. These traditions include the command to keep Sabbath rest, the promises to Abraham, the promise to David and his descendents, and the vision of the Jubilee and the restoration of Israel from the prophet Isaiah, especially those chapters that scholars assign to "Third" Isaiah (Isaiah 56–66). Moreover, the Sabbatical and Jubilee Years, especially as laid out in Deuteronomy 15, seem to be of particular importance for Luke's social vision for his community.[26] I look at each of these traditions in turn in this chapter, and then explore how Luke weaves one of these traditions, the Sabbatical Year, through several stories in both of his volumes so that it becomes a major theme supporting his project of redescription.

24. For a discussion of the interplay of social interests and mythmaking in the service of social formation, see Mack, *Myth and the Christian Nation*, 48–119.

25. Sanders, "On the Question of Method," 10. See also the discussion of how midrash functions in Callaway, *Sing O Barren One*, 5–12. Sanders suggests that the author of Luke draws upon this ancient practice of biblical reflection as he composes his two-volume work on the life of Jesus and the life of the church: "Luke's knowledge of Scripture apparently came from assiduous reading . . . he knew certain parts of scripture in such depth that unless the modern interpreter also knows the Septuagint . . . very well indeed he or she will miss major points Luke wanted to score. Those portions were centrally the Torah and the Deuteronomic history, that is, Genesis to 4 Kingdoms (2 Kings). Those sections of Scripture not only helped shape Luke's understanding of what God was doing in Christ (the Gospel) and in the early church (Acts), it also helped shape Luke's two-volume report of that activity." Sanders, "Isaiah in Luke," 16–17.

26. The connection between Deuteronomy 15 and the Bent-Over Woman is made by Evans, "Central Section of St. Luke's Gospel," 37–53. See especially 46. His article proposes that Luke has patterned his unusual central section (Luke 9:51—18:14) on Deuteronomy 12–26.

The Sabbath and the Sabbatical Year

The most obvious element of the Jewish mythic world upon which the story focuses is the commandment to keep the Sabbath holy. However, the emphasis on this commandment immediately introduces a level of ambiguity into the story, for the fourth commandment is unique in that the tradition provides two different rationales for observing it. The Priestly tradition (Exod 20:8–11) gives as the rationale for keeping Sabbath that God created the heavens and the earth in six days and on the seventh rested, and Israel is to do the same on every seventh day. The Deuteronomic tradition (Deut 5:12–15), however, gives as the rationale that God released Israel from slavery in Egypt, and in memory of that experience Israel is to rest every seventh day. As I have suggested above, given how Luke shapes his story, it seems likely that he is emphasizing the Deuteronomic rationale. He may, however, expect his hearers to have in the back of their minds the Exodus version of the commandment, since the disagreement between the synagogue leader and Jesus seems to rest on which rationale one chooses as the reason to observe the Sabbath, with the synagogue leader focusing on the Exodus rationale, while Jesus emphasizes the Deuteronomic rationale.

But why does Luke feel the need to include a Sabbath controversy story about a woman, when he has already introduced the Sabbath controversy story about the man with the withered hand from his Markan source (Mark 3:1–6//Luke 6:6–11), that explains why it is lawful to do good on the Sabbath? Why does he use here a rationale that is almost the same as the rationale that he will use in just a few verses, when he justifies the healing of the man with dropsy on the Sabbath (Luke 14:1–6), which reads: "Which of you, having a son or an ox that has fallen into a well, will not immediately pull him out on a Sabbath day?" (Luke 14:5// Matt 12:11–12).[27]

It is in that "almost the same" that the key lies, I believe. The question that is posed in the Sabbath controversies involving men is whether it is lawful (ἔξεστιν) to heal on the Sabbath, and does not include any notion of bondage from which the afflicted person is freed. As we have

---

27. For an in-depth discussion of this passage, see Braun, *Feasting and Social Rhetoric in Luke 14,* especially 22–42. It is noteworthy that Matthew uses this same rationale in his story of the man with the withered hand, which reads: "What man of you, if he has one sheep and it falls into a pit on the Sabbath, will not lay hold of it and lift it out? Of how much more value is a man than a sheep!" (Matt 12:11–12).

seen in the story of the Bent-Over Woman, however, the question is not about what one can or cannot do *legally* on the Sabbath, but rather about what one is *obligated* to do. By having Jesus recount who is required to observe the Sabbath, in concert with the use of a verb of liberation rather than healing, Luke alludes to the Deuteronomic rationale for keeping the Sabbath: The Israelites were once in bondage in Egypt, and God redeemed them from slavery (Deut 5:15). One is thus obligated to release those in bondage on the Sabbath because that is what God did for Israel.

With this rationale in mind, the intersection of Sabbath, daughters, and slaves with the verb ἀπολύω ("to be set free") should call to mind the legislation in Exodus 21 which uses this specific verb in its discussion of the obligation to release debt slaves in the Sabbatical Year—including provisions regarding daughters—and which follows directly on the heels of the enumeration of the Decalogue in Exodus 20.[28] Once this version of the Sabbatical Year release law is in view, a whole host of other legislation in the Septuagint regarding both the Sabbatical and Jubilee Years becomes the imaginative landscape against which this story is likely to be heard by Luke's audience.[29] In telling the woman she has been set free from bondage, calling her a daughter of Abraham, and in justifying his actions by alluding to the Deuteronomic rationale for observing the commandment, Luke's Jesus is able to expand the topic under discussion from what it is necessary to do on the Sabbath (rest) to what it is necessary to do during the Sabbatical Year: liberate Hebrew male and female slaves.

Promises to Abraham

One of the singular aspects of the story of the Bent-Over Woman is Luke's description of the woman as a "daughter of Abraham" (v.16). Luke seems to be the only biblical author to use this particular ascription. Jewish biblical tradition includes "daughter of Zion" (Lamentations, etc.), "daughters of Jerusalem (Song of Songs and elsewhere, including Luke 23:28), even "daughter of Sodom" and "daughter of Samaria" (Ezekiel 16),

---

28. Let me note that the requirements for the release of daughters in the Exodus 21 passage is quite different from that of male slaves, or of male and female slaves in the other Sabbatical Year texts such as Deuteronomy 15. I will be exploring this difference in more detail in the next chapter.

29. See Exod 21:2–11; Deut 15:1–18; Lev 25:1–55 as examples.

but nowhere is there the use of the phrase, "daughter of Abraham." The closest near usage is a passage from 4 Maccabees 15:28, "the daughter of the God-fearing Abraham," referring to the mother who supports her seven sons in choosing martyrdom over life at the hand of the Seleucid ruler Antiochus IV Epiphanes.[30] I will explore in more detail the social connotations of "daughter" in the next chapter; what I want to draw the reader's attention to in this chapter is the description of the woman as a child/descendent of Abraham. This description then brings into view the promises made to Abraham and his descendents, which are part of the mythic world of Judaism.

In Genesis 12, the first promise God makes to Abraham is that he will become "a great nation" (12:2), quickly followed by the promise to give these "offspring" the land of Canaan (12:7). In Genesis 15 the promise is repeated, although this time Abraham's offspring will be as numerous as the stars in the heaven (15:5). In Genesis 17, God returns to Abraham and repeats the promise; this time, however, Abraham will be the ancestor of "many nations" and the covenant that God is making will be not only with Abraham, but also "with his offspring through their generations, from everlasting to everlasting" (17:5–7). Finally, God promises a son, Isaac, who will be born to Abraham and Sarah; the covenant that God will make with Isaac will also be an everlasting covenant through the generations of his descendents (17:19). God's promises to Abraham thus give Abraham's descendents a place in the world and an eternal future, as well as a covenantal relationship with the divine.[31]

Luke is not the only author in the New Testament to make use of the Abraham tradition in his writings, of course.[32] James uses him as the exemplar for faith made visible through works (James 2:21–23), while the writer of Hebrews sees him as the example of faithful obedience

30. Sir Lancelot Charles Lee Brenton, in his 1851 edition of the Septuagint, does translate this verse as "But this *daughter of Abraham* remembered his holy fortitude." See Brenton, *The Septuagint with Apocrypha.*

31. Note that these social interests are similar to those identified by Burton Mack as comprising the social mentality supported by a society's mythic system (Mack, *Myth and the Christian Nation,* 52–73).

32. Using Abraham is not unique to "Christian" writers in the late and post–Second Temple period, of course. Philo has several treatises on Abraham, Josephus discusses his expertise as a general in his *Jewish Antiquities*, Ben Sira includes him among the honored ancestors, and, as has been noted above, Abraham's fear of God is seen as an example of strength analogous to the martyred mother and her seven sons in 4 Macc 15.

(Heb 11:8–19). Paul uses the Abraham tradition in Galatians 3 and in Romans 4 to establish a "kinship by faith" between his Gentile audience and Abraham as the father of Israel.[33]

Luke, according to Nils A. Dahl, uses Abraham as the touchstone for a "prophecy and fulfillment" motif running throughout the narrative of Luke-Acts. Dahl sees the major interpretive moment of this motif in the speech of Stephen in Acts 7: "Here God's word to Abraham is seen as the beginning of a history in which partial realizations are interconnected with new promises, until the coming of the Righteous One, of whom all the prophets spoke . . . the promise given to Abraham and now fulfilled in Jesus, first and foremost belonged to Abraham's posterity, circumcised Jews living in the land of Israel."[34]

---

33. Paul's major imaginative contribution to the development of Christianity is to assert that by virtue of Abraham having faith before the law was instituted (Rom 4:9–25; Gal 3:6–9; passim), it is possible for Gentiles to claim that they, too, are heirs of the promises made to Abraham, without having to abide by the provisions of the law (e.g., circumcision). For a superb exploration of the notion of fictive kinship in Paul, see Johnson Hodge, *If Sons, Then Heirs.*

34. Dahl, "Story of Abraham in Luke-Acts," 144, 147. Dahl's exegesis of Stephen's speech is illuminating, especially in his discussion of Acts 7:44–50, which recalls David's request of God to be allowed to build God's permanent house. This task is left to Solomon, and yet, according to Acts 7:48, "the Most High does not dwell in houses made with human hands." Dahl's contention is that this section of the speech does not reflect a radical anti-temple polemic, as some commentators have suggested; rather, this section refers to the "true" worshippers of God in Jerusalem, who understand the fulfillment of the promises made to Abraham as being fulfilled in Jesus of Nazareth; Stephen is presented as the true worshipper *par excellence* in Acts 7 (ibid., 145–47). As I will discuss in chapter 4 below, I suspect that part of what Luke is negotiating through the Bent-Over Woman pericope is exactly that: who constitutes the "true" Israel? Dahl also notes one curious omission in Luke's usage of the Abraham tradition in Stephen's speech that other NT writers do refer to: the binding of Isaac (ibid., 142). Elie Wiesel observes about Christianity's use of the binding Isaac, ". . . the threat hanging over Isaac is seen as a prefiguration of the crucifixion. Except that on Mount Moriah the act was *not* consummated: the father did *not* abandon his son. Such is the distance between Moriah and Golgotha" (Wiesel, *Messengers of God,* 67, emphasis in original). Wiesel reminds us that the midrashim on the binding of Isaac bring Satan into the picture; as in the case of Job, the midrashim assert that Satan is the one who makes God test Abraham's faithfulness by encouraging God to boast that even if God were to ask Abraham to sacrifice his son, Abraham would obey. For a discussion of the psychological aspects of the Akedah, as well as the texts of the midrashim on Genesis 22, see Dreifuss, "The Figures of Satan and Abraham," 166–78. One wonders whether the author of Luke had the binding of Isaac in mind when he described the woman as "bound by Satan," and to what extent her release is designed to recall for his audience the release of Isaac in Genesis 22. As Wiesel has noted, Jesus will *not* experience release from his captivity at the hands of

Dahl does give a brief nod to the "children of Abraham" as a motif in Luke, noting that calling the Bent-Over Woman a daughter of Abraham (Luke 13:16) strengthens Jesus' case for performing a Sabbath healing. He then suggests that this story, in partnership with John's prediction that the stones could be raised up as children of Abraham (Luke 3:8) and Jesus' affirmation that Zacchaeus has received salvation because he is a son of Abraham (Luke 19:9), "illustrate how God's promise to Abraham was fulfilled to his children through Jesus' ministry."[35]

Dahl seems to see this motif mostly as an afterthought, however, and fails to notice that in the story of the Bent-Over Woman, the promises to Abraham and the promises to David are woven together and embodied in the woman's experience of liberation. Through Luke's depiction of the woman being raised up (ἀνορθόω) in the same way in which YHWH promises that David's throne will be raised up in his descendents, and by Jesus' assertion that the woman must be set free on the Sabbath because she is a daughter of Abraham (and therefore part of the covenant people who are obligated to keep Sabbath), Luke's audience is likely to hear echoes of other passages in the gospel in which these themes are found. The two primary passages are Mary's song of praise (Luke 1:47–55), in which Abraham and his posterity receive God's help from generation to generation; and Zechariah's song (Luke 1:68–79), in which God has visited and redeemed God's people, because of "the oath which he swore to our father Abraham" (v.73). Moreover, Zechariah also explicitly mentions that God "has raised up the horn of salvation . . . in the house of his servant David" (v. 69), which, while not using the exact vocabulary of the Bent-Over Woman pericope, certainly uses these two traditions from Judaism's mythic world in order to bring both sets of promises together to reflect on God's actions in Zechariah's own time. The logic of Zechariah's song thus leads to the conclusion that the promises to Abraham are confirmed in the promise given to David; the experience of the Bent-Over Woman embodies the fulfillment of these expectations. Let me turn now to examine in more detail how Luke alludes to the promise to David in the Bent-Over-Woman story.

Pilate; as I will argue in chapter 4, the Bent-Over Woman's story is linked to Jesus' story of captivity by Luke through the use of ἀπολύω in both stories.

35. Dahl, "Story of Abraham," 150.

Promise to David

David is the recipient of one major promise from God: that the throne of his descendents will be established forever. This promise is recorded twice in the Hebrew Bible: in 2 Samuel 7:1–17 and the parallel passage in 1 Chronicles 17:1–15. Here is the promise as recorded in 2 Samuel 7: 11b–13, 16:

> 7:11b Moreover the Lord declares to you that the Lord will make you a house. When your days are fulfilled and you lie down with your ancestors, I will raise up your offspring after you, who shall come forth from your body, and I will establish his kingdom. He shall build a house for my name, and I will establish (ἀνορθώσω) the throne of his kingdom forever . . . 16 Your house and your kingdom shall be made sure forever before me; and your throne shall be established (ἀνωρθωμένος) forever.

James A. Sanders has suggested that Luke uses the technique of "word-tallying" as a way to make connections among biblical texts to support his theological agenda. Sanders notes, "In the first century, it was not uncommon to pull two or more passages out of their original literary contexts and read them together . . . Both passages would have had in them at least one word that was the same."[36] Although Sanders discusses this technique in regard to Jesus' reading from the Isaiah scroll in Luke 4 (see further discussion below), I am arguing that Luke also has used it in the Bent-Over Woman pericope as he describes the Woman's "straightening" with the verb ἀνορθόω. The term is quite unusual to describe the cure of a disability; I will explore just how unusual Luke's construction of the Woman's physical condition is in the next chapter. It is important to note here that his usage of ἀνορθόω is likely to bring to mind in his audience's imagination a key feature of the Jewish mythic world—YHWH's promise to David that a throne would be "raised up" and held by his descendents forever.[37]

36. Sanders, "Isaiah in Luke," 21.

37. God's promise to David of this eternal throne for his descendents is, of course, the basis for Jewish messianic ideologies that shape Christianity's understanding of Jesus as the Messiah. For thorough explorations of these ideologies at the end of the Second Temple period, see the collection of essays in Neusner, Green, and Frerichs, eds., *Judaisms and Their Messiahs,* and the collection of essays in Charlesworth, ed., *The Messiah.*

The term ἀνορθόω is used 15 times in the Septuagint: 2 Sam 7:13, 16//1 Chr 17:12, 14, 24; 1 Chr 22:10; Jer 10:12; Jer 40:2 (LXX); Ps 18: 35; Ps 20:8; Ps 144:14 (LXX); Ps 145:8 (LXX); Pr 24:3; Ezek 16:17: and Sir 27:14).[38] In a majority of the uses in the Septuagint the term is used in describing how YHWH will save Israel.[39] The critical utilizations of the word that I suspect Luke had in mind, however, are the parallel passages in 2 Samuel and 1 Chronicles. In a corrective vision given to the prophet Nathan, David is instructed not to build a permanent house for YHWH; instead, that task will be given to David's descendent, whose throne, as the Samuel text quoted above indicates, YHWH will "set up" (ἀνορθώσω ἀνωρθωμένος) forever. In Acts 15:15–18, Luke will use this same meaning of ἀνορθόω when James gives the final approval for Paul and Barnabas' mission to the Gentiles:

> This agrees with the prophets, as it is written,
> "After this I will return,
> and I will rebuild the dwelling of David, which has fallen;
> From its ruins I will rebuild it,
> and I will set it up (ἀνορθώσω),
> So that all other peoples may seek the Lord—
> even all the Gentiles over whom my names has been called."
> Thus says the Lord, who has been making these things known
> from long ago.

James is here depicted as quoting a passage from Amos 9:11–12. However, ἀνορθώσω is not the verb used in Amos; rather ἀνοικοδομέω is the verb in the Septuagint as we have it, suggesting that Luke has edited the quotation in order to make the linkage with the promise given to David in Samuel and Chronicles.[40]

---

38. Hamm, "Freeing," 28.

39. The use of the term in Proverbs 42:3 is similar to that in the majority of the usages relating somehow to YHWH's salvation of Israel : "A house is built by wisdom and is set up (ἀνορθοῦται) by understanding." In two instances, however, ἀνορθόω is used to describe body parts that stand upright: in Sirach 27:14, the hair on one's head "stands upright" in the company of one who swears too much, while in Ezek 16:7b Jerusalem's breasts are described as 'upright' (ἀνωρθώθησαν), indicating that Jerusalem is of marriageable age as God enters into covenant with her. This passage is a rather disturbing tirade against Jerusalem's whoring (=idolatrous) tendencies, along with her sisters, Sodom and Samaria.

40. Hamm, "Freeing," 33.

Turid Karlsen Seim has argued against seeing a strong linkage between the use of ἀνορθόω in Luke 13:13 and Acts 15:16. She says,

> The suggestion that the verb ἀνορθόω in 13:13 is to be associated with the use of the same verb in Acts 15:16 demands that the healing of the woman bent double is taken as a symbolic expression for the reconstruction of Israel in the group of those who believe in Jesus. The designation "Abraham's daughter" would then have the same corporative symbolic meaning as in some rabbinic texts. Quite apart from the fact that the connection between the two passages is extremely slender, this interpretation completely overlooks the value of the narrative in Luke 13:10–17 as a concretisation. At the same time, it is correct in pointing to its exemplary significance.[41]

I would argue, however, that because of the comparatively consistent use of the term in the Septuagint in referring to God's acts of salvation, particularly in regard to the restoration of the house of David, and because Luke uses it in the sense of the establishment and restoration of David's throne in Acts, it is far more likely that Luke is assuming his hearers will have this symbolic understanding of the term in mind when they hear the story of the Bent-Over Woman.[42] The question this linkage raises, then, is what does Luke suggest by associating this woman—this child of Abraham—with the restoration of David's throne? Before answering this question, let us explore another theme from Luke's mythic world, the vision of God's restoration and re-creation of Israel in Isaiah 55–66, which seems to be echoed in the story of the Bent-Over Woman.

Isaiah's Vision of Israel's Restoration

In the story of the Bent-Over Woman, Luke's audience may well have heard echoes from the final sections of Isaiah (chapters 55–66), which collects many images of Israel's restoration following the Babylonian exile. Many of these chapters address what the appropriate keeping of the Sabbath involves (e.g., Isa 58), and what benefits will accrue to those who keep it faithfully, including those persons who have traditionally

41. Seim, *Double Message,* 54.

42. The term ἀνορθόω is used one other time in the New Testament; in Heb 12:12, the faithful are enjoined to "strengthen your weak knees" so that "what is lame may not be put out of joint but rather healed (12:13b). This is an intriguing juxtaposition of healing and disability, although other than ἀνορθόω, the vocabulary used is quite different from Luke's vocabulary in Luke 13:10–17.

been thought of as outside the covenant tradition (e.g., foreigners and eunuchs in Isa 56:1–8). Given that Luke is presumably writing after the destruction of Jerusalem by Rome in 73 CE, the visions of the prophet of Third Isaiah in which Jerusalem is vindicated before all the nations (e.g., Isa 62:1–2) and is restored as a city of persons gathered from many nations (e.g., Isa 56:6–8) may have offered Luke's audience a way to understand their own mixed gathering.[43]

Furthermore, because the Bent-Over Woman pericope is a Sabbath story in which Jesus is teaching in a synagogue, Luke's hearers may also be expected to have in mind other synagogue stories Luke tells about Jesus. The one with the closest parallels is the story of Jesus in the synagogue at Nazareth, which is at the beginning of Jesus' ministry in Luke 4:16–21; as it turns out, the story of Jesus and the Bent-Over Woman will be the last time we see Jesus in a synagogue in the gospel.

To have the Nazareth synagogue scene in mind as one encounters the Bent-Over Woman is immediately to have the words of the prophet Isaiah read by Jesus in the Nazareth synagogue called to mind. In this scene, Luke has used phrases from two different sections of Third Isaiah to create Jesus' reading from the Isaiah scroll: Isa 61:1–2 and Isa 58:6. Sanders suggests that Luke has used the technique of "word tallying" here to bring these two passages together thematically:

> Here it was the Greek word ἄφεσις, meaning release or forgiveness: to preach ἄφεσις to captives (Isa 61:1) and to send the oppressed in ἄφεσις (Isa 58:6). To get the full impact of the word tallying one must realize that ἄφεσις is the Greek translation of Hebrew *shemittah* in Deuteronomy 15 and Hebrew *deror* in Leviticus 25—the two passages in the Old Testament which provide legislation concerning the Jubilee Year. Luke's Jesus conjoined the two passages from Isaiah fully in the spirit and even the letter of Isaiah 61, which was itself composed out of Jubilee traditions.[44]

The woman's experience of liberation in her synagogue encounter with Jesus would thus bring to mind the earlier quotations from Isaiah presented during the scene in the Nazareth synagogue; furthermore, it seems

---

43. See also my discussion of the Bent-Over Woman as a possible allusion to the *Judea Capta* coins circulating throughout the Roman Empire following Jerusalem's destruction in chapter 4 below.

44. Sanders, "Isaiah in Luke," 21.

likely that the entire range of Jubilee traditions would be present in the imagination of Luke's audience in this story as well as in the Nazareth synagogue scene.[45]

These two Sabbath synagogue stories serve as bookends[46] to those situations by which Jesus' prophetic words and deeds are shown to be congruent: while Jesus says he has come to release captives in the Nazareth incident and that the prophecy of Isaiah is fulfilled that day in their hearing, in the encounter with the Bent-Over Woman he actually does release a captive, as he re-interprets the Woman's condition from illness to bondage. From the Nazareth synagogue on a Sabbath to this synagogue on a Sabbath somewhere on the way to Jerusalem, Luke has been weaving a theme of Jesus as the prophet whose words are fulfilled in the here and now, just as he claimed in Nazareth. In Isaiah 66:18, God says, "I know their works and their thoughts," an image that Luke will repeatedly apply to Jesus in the various engagements he has with the Pharisees and others between these two Sabbath stories.[47] This repetition serves to strengthen the characterization of Jesus as the "prophet like Moses," which will be one of the ways in which Peter will describe Jesus in his second speech to the "Israelites" in Acts 3:12–26.[48]

45. I will discuss the relationship between the Bent-Over Woman story and the legal provisions for observing the Jubilee Year in Leviticus 25 and 26 in chapter 3 below.

46. Here Luke may be employing imagery from Isaiah 66:23 as a literary device: "From new moon to new moon and Sabbath to Sabbath, all flesh shall come to worship before me, says the Lord."

47. The places where this phrasing occurs are: Luke 5:22 healing of the paralytic (also in Mark); 6:8 healing of the man with the withered hand (only in Luke); 7:39–40 Simon the Pharisee at the anointing (only in Luke); 9:47 dispute among the disciples about who is the greatest (only in Luke); 11:17 Beelzebul controversy (in Matt also); 20:23 the craftiness of the spies sent to catch him as he taught in the temple (all three). All of these incidents are paralleled in all three synoptic gospels; as I have indicated, in several of them only Luke includes a statement about Jesus "knowing" or "perceiving" what is in the other participants' inner thoughts. Except for the final one, all of these incidents fall within the Sabbath/synagogue to Sabbath/synagogue inclusio created by the pairing of the Nazareth synagogue scene and the synagogue scene with the Bent-Over Woman.

48. Aune suggests that Luke includes as a theme "the Prophet as an Endangered Species" in that "Luke's interest in the prophetic status of Jesus is connected with the motif of the violent fate of the prophets, i.e., the widespread Jewish view that suffering and martyrdom were inevitable for a true prophet . . . Jesus is rejected and killed, not *primarily* because his words and behavior antagonize Jewish authorities, but because he is a prophet of God" (Aune, *The New Testament in Its Literary Environment,* 132; emphasis in original).

A further connection between the two stories can be seen in Luke's use of Isaiah 58, from which Luke borrows to complete Jesus' Isaiah quotation. In addition to its description of the behavior God desires more than correct ritual behavior (e.g., to let the oppressed go free, to share your bread with the hungry, vv. 6–7), the passage also describes right behavior on the Sabbath (Isa 58:13–14). Furthermore, Isaiah 58 includes language that is reminiscent of Luke's language in the Bent-Over Woman story, in that bonds should be unloosed (λυε̂ . . . σύνδεσμον, v.6) so that Israel's foundations will last through all generations (Isa 58:12–14).[49]

So far we have the traditions of keeping Sabbath, the promises to Abraham, the promise to David, and the prophecies of Isaiah in play in the Bent-Over Woman story. Is Luke finished yet? I think not; there appears to be one additional theme that he has brought into play in this pericope, which further links this story to other stories in both Luke and Acts. I turn now to explore this final element of Luke's Mythic World that I see at work in the passage.

DEUTERONOMY 15 AS SOCIAL VISION BEHIND LUKE-ACTS

In her book, *Weaving Truth: Essays on Language and the Female in Greek Thought*, Ann Bergren notes,

> Greek culture inherits from Indo-European a metaphor by which poets and prophets define themselves as "weaving" or "sewing" words. That is, they describe their activity in terms of what is originally and literally, women's work par excellence. They call their product, in effect, a "metaphorical web." . . . Weaving has an intellectual counterpart in Greek. It is the skill known as [μῆτις . . . which] denotes throughout Greek thought the power of transformation . . .[50]

As we have seen already, Luke is an excellent weaver of words, capable of extending the pattern of his design not just across one book,

49. Hamm suggests an additional connection to Luke's use of Isaiah, this time from the section ascribed to "Second" Isaiah: the phrase κατῃσχύνοντο πάντες οἱ ἀντικεί μενοι αὐτῷ (all his adversaries were put to shame, Luke 13:17a), which seems to be an allusion to Isa 45:16 LXX. Hamm sees this allusion as an example of the conjoining of the creative and redemptive activity of God, in that the oracle speaks both of the creation of the earth, the heavens, and humankind (Isa 45:12) as well as the raising up of Cyrus who will build YHWH's city and set YHWH's exiles free (Isa 45:13). Hamm, "Freeing," 27–28.

50. Bergren, *Weaving Truth*, 16–17.

but across two. To see his μῆτις at work even more completely, I use the method of intertextuality as outlined by Paul Ricouer in his article "The Bible and the Imagination." Ricoeur proposes that reading the Bible is an imaginative act, a "creative operation that is constantly decontextualizing and recontextualizing the meanings of a biblical text in today's Sitz-im-Leben."[51] He goes on to suggest that the intersection between text and life is what stimulates the imagination of one reading the Bible; the act of reading should be seen as the junction of "itineraries of meaning" found in the text that have the power to redescribe reality for the reader.[52]

Ricoeur uses the process of 'intertextuality' in his article to explore the relationship between two of the kingdom parables in the gospel of Mark and the larger narrative structure within which they are embedded.[53] He defines intertextuality as the way in which "one text in referring to another text both displaces this other text and receives from it an extension of meaning."[54] Ricoeur suggests that a fuller set of meanings can be discovered when one looks at the parables in this way, rather than focusing on them only as individual pericopae that are distinct from the larger literary context which encompasses them, as do many historical-critical approaches to biblical exegesis.[55] This fuller set of meanings is what Ricoeur terms "metaphorization"—the way in which the parables become something more than simply tales about vineyard owners and sowers of seeds, by helping the reader to learn something, not only about what the kingdom of God is like, but also something about the one who tells the tales (Jesus).[56]

Ricoeur suspects that intertextuality can also expand the itineraries of meaning for non-parabolic narratives in the gospels and the Bible as a whole; he invites other interpreters of scripture to take up that exploration, and it is that invitation that I accept in this section. Intertextuality offers an interpretive process for making additional sense of the Bent-Over Woman story by seeing the literary connections between her story and that of the Woman who Anoints Jesus in Luke 7:36–50. Furthermore, by

51. Ricoeur, "Bible and the Imagination," 145.

52. Ibid., 146.

53. The parable of the wicked tenants (Mark 12: 1–12) and the parable of the sower (Mark 4:1–9).

54. Ricoeur, "Bible and the Imagination," 148.

55. Ibid., 149.

56. Ibid.

seeing these two stories in light of Luke's redaction of the Lord's Prayer, his rationale for reworking the anointing story and for including the Bent-Over Woman in the gospel becomes clearer: the two women can be understood as metaphors for the community that prays this prayer. For Luke, it appears that this community is the one that embodies the social vision of Deuteronomy 15, which requires the forgiveness of debts and the release of Hebrew slaves in the seventh year.

The two stories have had very different scholarly histories. Because an anointing of Jesus is found in each of the four canonical gospels, much scholarly work has focused on the various versions of the story.[57] Luke's version, which is removed from the Passion Narrative in order to come earlier in the plotline of his gospel narrative, describes the anointing of Jesus' feet rather than his head, and includes a parable by Jesus about two debtors. It has often been thought to come from a different tradition than the source of the version found in the other three gospels. To the contrary, Kathleen E. Corley and Burton L. Mack argue convincingly that there is a single story behind all four versions, which has been redacted to serve the various purposes of each canonical gospel writer.[58]

The Bent-Over Woman, on the other hand, is found only in Luke's gospel, and therefore has received very little scholarly attention. As I have argued above, however, this story is a carefully crafted elaboration of a *chreia*, designed to move forward Luke's goals for his literary composition. I will first examine the anointing story, then review the Bent-Over Woman story, and finally look at the two stories intertextually in light of Luke's version of the Lord's Prayer, in order to see what new itineraries of meaning we may discover by looking at the three texts together.

THE ANOINTING OF JESUS: LUKE 7:36–50

Kathleen Corley has summarized the common elements behind all four of the anointing stories in the gospel tradition:

1. Jesus is anointed with expensive perfume by a woman
2. The anointing takes place in the context of a meal
3. Others present at the meal object to her action
4. Jesus rises to defend her.[59]

---

57. For a representative discussion of the history of scholarship on the anointing story see Corley, "Anointing of Jesus in the Synoptic Tradition," 61–72.

58. Ibid., 62–63. See also Mack, "Anointing of Jesus," 85–92.

59. Corley, "Anointing in the Synoptic tradition," 61.

In Mark, Matthew, and John, the story is related as part of the extended Passion narrative, and like the Bent-Over Woman, takes the form of an elaborated *chreia*.[60] The woman's action in these versions is described by Jesus as "good" (καλός) because she has anointed Jesus' body for burial; the objection that the woman has wasted the perfume on Jesus is countered by Jesus' quotation of Deuteronomy 15:11 that there will always be poor in the land. The logic of the argumentation is thus grounded in a hierarchy of Jewish good deeds: almsgiving could be done at any time, because "the poor are always with you," but burial of the dead had to be done when it was needed, and therefore had a higher priority. But what is also at stake—at least for Mark and Matthew—is Jesus' status as the Christ, the anointed one of God; the woman stands in the place of Samuel anointing David beforehand as the one chosen by God to be the "true" king of Israel (1 Sam 16:1–13). In Mark and Matthew, the woman's action of anointing Jesus will be confirmed by the Roman centurion during the crucifixion scene.[61]

Because Luke has depicted Jesus' anointing by the Spirit at the time of his baptism, and had Jesus claim this anointing of the Spirit in his "inaugural" sermon in Nazareth, the story of Jesus' anointing by a woman from his Markan source is available to him for other rhetorical purposes. In Luke's version of the story, Jesus is invited to the home of a Pharisee, rather than a leper (as in Mark and Matthew), whom we only later discover is also named Simon. The objection to the woman's action is no longer the waste of the ointment but her reputation in the community as a sinner (ἁμαρτωλός); Simon questions—to himself—Jesus' status as a prophet because he allows the woman to touch him. Jesus responds to Simon's unspoken objection (thus refuting Simon's doubt regarding Jesus' prophetic status) by telling a parable about two debtors whose debts are forgiven, and then by contrasting the woman's actions with Simon's lack of hospitality; he concludes by telling the woman that her sins have been forgiven. Other guests suddenly make an appearance, also questioning Jesus' identity and his claim to have authority to forgive the woman's sins. Jesus' final comment to the woman is that her faith

60. Mack, "Anointing of Jesus," 85–106.

61. In Mark, the Roman centurion will say, "Truly this man was the Son of God!" (Mark 15:39//Matt 27:54), which implicitly means "King of Israel." For a full discussion of the nuances of this argument, see Mack, "The Anointing of Jesus," 92–100. See also Elisabeth Schüssler Fiorenza's discussion of the anointing as prophetic sign-act in Schüssler Fiorenza, *In Memory of Her*, xiii–xiv.

has saved her; she is encouraged to go in peace. To summarize, Luke has changed the story in the following ways:

1. The location is now Galilee rather than Bethany.

2. The timing is now earlier in Jesus ministry, rather than in the final week.

3. The host is now a Pharisee, rather than either a leper or Martha, the sister of Lazarus and Mary.

4. The woman anoints Jesus' feet rather than his head (also in John).

5. The objection is about Jesus' identity rather than the waste of the ointment.

6. Jesus tells a parable, rather than quoting scripture.

7. The woman is presented as the true host, while Simon is portrayed as a host lacking in hospitality.

8. The result of the anointing is an acknowledgement that the woman's sins have been forgiven, rather than that Jesus' body has been anointed for burial.

The parable is what strikes the ear as odd; why does Jesus tell a parable about two debtors, if the woman is a sinner (with all the sexual overtones implied by the appellation "of the city")? What connection is Luke making between forgiveness of sins and forgiveness of debts, beyond the obvious connection of magnitude? Here Luke's skill as a rhetorician comes to the fore; he takes Jesus' reference to Deuteronomy 15:11 in Mark 14:7, and turns it into a parable that reflects on the first half of Deuteronomy 15, which deals with the forgiveness of debts in the Sabbatical Year. In particular, Luke seems to be elaborating Deuteronomy 15: 9, which says,

> Take heed to yourself, that wickedness not be born secretly in your heart, saying, "The seventh year, the year of release approaches," and your eye look with evil upon your brother who is in need, and you give him nothing, and he cry out against you to [the] Lord, and there will be great sin (ἁμαρτία μεγάλη) in you.[62]

The host, presented by Luke as a Pharisee, someone knowledgeable in the law, should immediately hear echoes of the Deuteronomic Sabbatical

---

62. Author's translation from the Septuagint.

Year legislation in this parable of great debt forgiven. He might also hear echoes of Leviticus 6:1–7, which discusses the penalty and guilt offering required in restitution for sinning against God by deceiving a neighbor in the matter of a deposit or a pledge, or by defrauding a neighbor.

But there is a further twist. Jesus asks Simon which of the debtors will love the creditor more; when Simon replies (rather grudgingly!) "The one to whom he forgave more," Jesus affirms his answer with language we will hear echoed again after Jesus' telling of the parable of the Good Samaritan in chapter 10: "you have judged rightly" (Luke 7:43). In Luke 10:25–37 we meet a lawyer who asks Jesus what he must do to inherit eternal life; when Jesus asks him what is written in the law, the lawyer responds, "You shall love the Lord your God with all your heart and with all your soul, and with all your strength, and with all your mind, and your neighbor as yourself" (Luke 10:27). Just as he affirmed Simon's response, Jesus affirms the lawyer's response: "you have answered rightly" (v. 28). But the lawyer doesn't leave the discussion there; instead he asks, "Who is my neighbor?" Jesus' reply is, of course, the parable of the Good Samaritan. It is noteworthy that the definition of neighbor (πλησίον), used in Deut 15:2 and further identified as "brother" (αδελφός) in Deut 15: 3, is here expanded to include those who are excluded (foreigners = Samaritans) as neighbors in Deut 15:3.[63]

Keeping the notion of intertextuality in mind, we can see some surprising displacements and extensions of meaning in Luke's version of the anointing of Jesus:

1. By reworking his Markan source through the use of a parable, Luke's hearers are reminded of the Sabbatical Year forgiveness of debts, which refers not just to the poor but also to one's neighbors;

2. By having Jesus ask who loves more, Luke refers proleptically to the summary of the law that will be given by the lawyer in chapter 10;

3. By having the lawyer ask, "who is my neighbor?" we see an expansion of the definition of neighbor in the gospel to include those who

63. One notes that the Samaritan responds in the moment to the need of the man before him (just as Jesus will affirm the woman's action in anointing him in the Markan story), while the priest and the Levite may have avoided dealing with the man (who appears to be dead) in order to be able to fulfill their cultic responsibilities. Since he doesn't use it in his version of the anointing, one wonders whether Luke has transposed the argument about when one is called upon to fulfill acts of charity to the parable of the Good Samaritan.

are outside of the community of Israel, which potentially extends the definition of the community of neighbors that participates in the Sabbatical Year forgiveness of debts;

4. By linking debts, neighbors, and sins, Luke also calls to mind the legal provisions of Leviticus 6:1–7, which will be embodied later in the gospel (Luke 19:1–10) through the story of Zacchaeus, whom Jesus names "son of Abraham," a parallel construction to the "daughter of Abraham" in the Bent-Over Woman narrative.[64]

The Bent-Over Woman: Luke 13:10–17

Let us review briefly our findings about the story of the Bent-Over Woman, in order to see its connections to the story of the Woman who Anoints Jesus. As I have already discussed, the verb used by Jesus to describe what has happened to the Bent-Over Woman is not a verb of healing, but instead is associated with the release of slaves in the Sabbatical Year (ἀπολύω). By his unusual use of this verb, Luke calls to mind the legislation about the release of debt slaves—specifically including daughters—in Exodus 21:1–11, which uses a form of this same verb. Luke further calls upon the Deuteronomic rationale for keeping the Sabbath: Israel was once in bondage in Egypt, and God redeemed them from slavery (Deut 5:15). By telling the woman she has been set free using a verb from a Sabbatical Year text, Luke's Jesus is able to broaden the topic under discussion from what is necessary on the Sabbath to what is necessary during the Sabbatical Year: the liberation of Hebrew male and female slaves. Jesus' response thus overcomes in a surprising way the synagogue leader's challenge, which equated the act of healing the woman with work that is prohibited by the command to keep Sabbath rest.[65]

---

64. Of course, the first time Luke's community heard or read the gospel they might not make the connections between these stories; however, as the gospel was read again and again, the extension of meanings between the texts may well have become more clear, while at the same time stronger connections were being made between the life of Jesus and the Scriptures of Israel with which the audience seems to be familiar—the Septuagint.

65. Halvor Moxnes focuses on the notion of honor and shame in this passage, proposing that this story is really about the argument (challenge-riposte) between Jesus and the synagogue leader. Interestingly, in his discussion, the Woman is completely invisible. Moxnes, "Honor and Shame," especially 22–23.

As I have suggested above, however, there is clearly more going on in the story than just another report of Jesus overcoming a challenge posed by a religious leader. If we use intertextuality to listen for other relationships, there are a number of additional passages in the gospel that come to mind. As I have already discussed, Luke links this story to the first time we see Jesus teaching in a synagogue, in Nazareth.[66] In addition, we are told that the woman is "bent over and quite unable to stand up straight" (Luke 13:11b). After Jesus announces her liberation and lays his hands on her, "immediately" she stands up straight and begins praising God (Luke 13:12b–13). In her transformation, therefore, she embodies John the Baptist's proclamation at the beginning of the gospel that the crooked shall be made straight (Luke 3:5c). Furthermore, Jesus' liberation of the woman and besting of the synagogue leader's challenge embodies Mary's earlier affirmation in her song that the powerful shall be brought low, and the lowly shall be lifted up (Luke 1:52). And, in alluding to the release of Hebrew slaves in the Sabbatical Year as an underlying justification for Jesus' liberation of the woman on the Sabbath, Luke brings us back again to Deuteronomy 15. Here, however, Luke calls on the latter part of the chapter:

> If a member of your community, whether a Hebrew man or a Hebrew woman, is sold to you and works for you for six years, in the seventh year you shall set that person free . . . Remember that you were a slave in the land of Egypt, and the Lord your God redeemed you; for this reason I lay this command upon you today. (Deut 15:12, 15)

The Bent-Over Woman, described by Jesus as a daughter of Abraham, should clearly be seen as a Hebrew woman whom God expected to be freed in the Sabbatical Year; having been held captive for 18 years, she is long overdue for liberation.[67]

---

66. It is important to note here that the Woman who anoints Jesus confirms the earlier part of the prophecy that Jesus reads in Nazareth: "The Spirit of the Lord is upon me, because he has *anointed* me . . ." (Luke 4:18a), which makes another connection between the two women stories.

67. Hamm cites J. D. M. Derrett's suggestion that the curious use of "18 years" to describe the length of time of the woman's captivity may be a reference to the two periods of 18 years in which Israel was held captive, recorded in Judges 3:14 and 10:8. (Hamm, "Freeing," 43 n. 43.) Mikeal C. Parsons suggests another intriguing possibility: the numerology representing the number 18—especially when spelled out as *deka kai oktō* (10 and 8) as it is in the second reference in the story—can be written using the

THE LORD'S PRAYER: LUKE 11:1–4

By his allusion to Deuteronomy 15:1–18 in both the anointing of Jesus and the liberation of the Bent-Over Woman, I believe Luke is inviting his readers to hold these two women together in their minds—but why? Here is where Luke's redaction of the Lord's Prayer provides a further interpretive key. The Lord's Prayer falls approximately halfway between the two women stories in Luke's narrative structure. It is considered by most scholars to be in the Q material shared by Luke and Matthew, although there are significant differences between the two versions.[68] One important difference, clearly due to the interests of each gospel writer, is the narrative setting of the prayer: in Matthew's gospel the prayer is presented as part of Jesus' teaching to the crowds during the Sermon on the Mount (Matt 6:7–13), while in Luke it is the disciples who have asked him to teach them to pray "as John taught his disciples" (Luke 11:1). Matthew's version is also longer, including one additional petition (Matt 6:10b) and adding a secondary clause to another (Matt 6:13b). But the petition that particularly concerns us is the petition related to forgiveness. Matthew records it as "Forgive us our debts, as we also have forgiven our debtors" (Matt 6:12). Luke, however, says, "Forgive us our sins, for we ourselves forgive everyone who is indebted to us" (Luke 11:4ab). In contrast to much of the rest of the Q material, in this instance it seems as though it is Matthew who retains the more original version and Luke who may have redacted both clauses of the petition to serve his literary and theological purposes.[69] Here are the two versions of the prayer from Luke and Matthew:

---

letters that signify the Greek numerals for 10 and 8: iota and epsilon. When written as ie with a line over it to signify the numerals, it also serves as an acronym for the *sacra nomen* (sacred name) of Jesus. Parsons, *Body and Character in Luke and Acts*, 89–95.

68. See John S. Kloppenborg, *Q Parallels*, 84, for a list of scholarly positions on whether it should be included in Q. See also the non-gospel parallels in ibid., 83.

69. Taussig, *Jesus before God*, 63.

TABLE 2: The Lord's Prayer in Luke and Matthew

Luke	Matthew
11:2 And he said to them, "When you pray, say: "Father, hallowed be your name. Your kingdom come.	6:9 Pray then like this: "Our Father in heaven, hallowed be your name. (10a) Your kingdom come, (10b) your will be done, on earth as it is in heaven.
11:3 Give us each day our daily bread,	6:11 Give us this day our daily bread,
11:4 and forgive us our sins, for we ourselves forgive everyone who is indebted to us. And lead us not into temptation."	6:12 and forgive us our debts, as we also have forgiven our debtors. (13a) And lead us not into temptation, (13b) but deliver us from evil.

Hal Taussig suggests that in the first clause of the petition about forgiveness, Luke is speaking about sins "in general."[70] My contention, however, is that Luke reworks the language about debts in order to refer to sins as he has presented them in the anointing story—sins linked to financial dealings through the parable about debtors in Luke 7:41–42, and therefore reminiscent of both the "great sin" of not forgiving debts in the Sabbatical Year in Deuteronomy 15:9 and the guilt offering in Leviticus 6. Luke may thus expect his hearers to remember the woman who anoints Jesus when they reach this passage about how Jesus' disciples are expected to pray.[71] Luke maintains the reference to debts in the second half of the petition from his Q source, but changes the nuances of the language. This change is suggestive of Deuteronomy 15, for one was expected in the Sabbatical Year to forgive the debts of all those who still had outstanding debts owed to one—as well as to release those who had sold themselves into slavery to pay off their debts. Luke is setting the stage for his hearers to remember the prayer—and the anointing—when they reach the story about the Bent-Over Woman. With the two women stories held together by the prayer—a prayer set up narratively by Luke specifically for Jesus' disciples to pray—Deuteronomy 15 as a whole

70. Ibid., 89.

71. Interestingly, when the community reaches the story of Zacchaeus later in the gospel, his actions in response to Jesus' visit will more than fulfill the provisions of the guilt offering, just as the community of Acts 4 will more than fulfill the provisions of Deuteronomy 15.

becomes available to the community (of disciples) as the model for how they should organize their life together.

We have seen that Luke cleverly links the association of debts and sins in his revision of the anointing; he uses that association to expand the "neighbor" to whom the commandment in Deuteronomy 15 applies by way of the parable of the Good Samaritan. The Bent-Over Woman helps to expand the concept of neighbor beyond even Samaritans, however; Jesus' argument in the story using the strategy of arguing from the lesser to the greater has reminded his hearers that the range of persons who are obligated by the commandment to keep Sabbath rest includes the "resident alien in your towns" (Exod 20:10b//Deut 5:14b). Luke thus sets the stage for the blessing of Deuteronomy 15 to fall upon the community in Acts that is made up of those who have responded affirmatively to Jesus' witnesses, not only in Jerusalem, but "in all Judea and Samaria, and to the ends of the earth" (Acts 1:8b).

Deuteronomy 15 specifies that the entire commandment must be kept in order for the blessing to be received; to make the passage truly look like their life together, therefore, Luke's community must be seen to both forgive debts and release slaves. Acts 4:32–35 says:

> Now the whole group of those who believed were of one heart and soul, and no one claimed private ownership of any possessions, but everything they owned was held in common. With great power the apostles gave their testimony to the resurrection of the Lord Jesus, and great grace was upon them all. There was not a needy person among them, for as many as owned lands or houses sold them and brought the proceeds of what was sold. They laid it at the apostles' feet, and it was distributed to each as any had need.

Luke's portrayal of the community in Acts thus goes beyond what was expected of the community in Deuteronomy 15; by bringing the proceeds from the sale of their possessions to be distributed among the community, those with possessions *prevent* the possibility that persons will have to sell themselves into slavery as a way to meet their debts.[72]

---

72. Luke does suggest there are dire consequences (death!) for not fulfilling the commandment in his story of the husband and wife team who conspire in keeping back some of the profits from property they had sold (Acts 5:1–11).

Conclusion

And so we come again to the question, what might Luke be inviting his audience to imagine with him, as he uses their shared mythic world to deposit layers and layers of tradition into this story of the Bent-Over Woman? To recap briefly, the setting of the story is a Sabbath day, on which Jesus' words and actions are questioned by someone in authority. Jesus' words and actions, which engage the woman directly, "enflesh" the prophecies from Isaiah he said had been fulfilled in the synagogue in Nazareth, and thereby invite the audience to bring to mind the various images of liberation, economic and social justice, and restoration which Isaiah prophesies for God's people in the portion of Isaiah from which these readings are drawn (Isaiah 55–66).

Jesus' rebuttal to the critique of his actions draws on the Deuteronomic tradition for observing the commandment to keep Sabbath rest, and is further strengthened by naming the woman as a "daughter of Abraham," clearly locating her within the covenant family. In doing so, Luke brings to mind the promises that Abraham received from God, that Abraham's descendents would be a people, in a place of their own, and in relationship with this God forever. Luke further cements in place the eternal nature of these promises by linking the woman's transformation to the throne of David's descendents, which God has promised to "establish" forever. Then Luke links this woman to a number of other passages in his first volume as well as in his second volume through the Sabbatical Year legislation of Deuteronomy 15, thereby prefiguring in her story how he will describe the post-Pentecost community of believers in this same Jesus of Nazareth. Whew! No wonder the woman is Bent-Over, with all these traditions piled on her back!

If, as Burton Mack suggests, myths "create a space for thinking critically about the present state of a group's life together," and also "stretch the imagination and work out theoretical questions" about a group's identity and place in a larger world,[73] what might Luke's manipulation of his group's mythic world suggest about the issues his group is concerned with? How might he be using this woman to "think with" his community about who Jesus is, and who they are, just as Mark seems to use the Syro-Phoenician Woman?

---

73. Mack, *Christian Myth*, 69.

Jesus' role seems to be established as the "prophet like Moses" (or perhaps the one who is even greater?) in that his words and deeds are congruent, and bear fruit in the present, not in some far off distant future. He is also God's Son, God's chosen one, to whom one is expected to listen (Luke 3:22, 9:35, Acts 3:22); if one does not, "you will be utterly rooted out of the people," according to Peter, who will bring these themes together in his speech to the "Men of Israel" at the temple in Acts 3:11–26.

As we turn our focus to the community, it seems as if they are concerned about their future, for both the Abraham and David traditions assert that those who can claim descent from Abraham and David are assured of an eternal future. The themes I have highlighted above suggest that the community may understand itself to be the manifestation of God's restoration of Israel, presumably in the wake of the destruction of the Jerusalem temple in 70 CE, which had happened at some time in the group's (perhaps distant) past. The Isaiah traditions used by Luke include the notion of release from oppression and bondage, a notion that is further supported by the Deuteronomic Sabbath observance and Sabbatical Year legislation that is grounded in Israel's release from bondage in Egypt. These traditions thus also suggest a concern about economic and social justice, in which God supports—and engages in—social reversal that upsets traditional ideologies of power.

Finally, the layering of these traditions suggest that Luke's social group is not entirely Jewish, although they must have enough familiarity with the Jewish scriptures for the text to make sense. Each tradition has somewhere in it a way in which the benefits become available to those who are not part of Israel, whether it is Abraham as the father of many nations (Gen 17:5), David's dwelling that will be re-established so that Gentiles may seek the Lord (Amos 9:12), the tradition in Isaiah that the foreigners who keep the Sabbath will be gathered to God's holy mountain (Isa 56:6–7), or the requirement that "resident aliens" be included among those who keep the Sabbath (Deut 5:14//Exod 20:10). One might also consider here the Exodus rationale for keeping Sabbath, which is grounded in God's act of creation; if God created everything, how could those outside of Israel not receive at least some form of blessing or benefit from their Creator?

I leave these possibilities in the air for now. We will return to their consideration in chapter 4, as we consider the findings not only of this chapter, but also of our exploration of Luke's Society and Culture Worlds, as we turn in the next chapter to consider the topography of Luke's Society World.

3

Bent Over and Bound No Longer

The Society and Culture Worlds of the Bent-Over Woman

INTRODUCTION

IN THIS CHAPTER, I will explore Luke 13:10–17 by applying the Society and Culture Worlds of the Social Imagination model to the pericope. The reader will remember that the Society World is, essentially, the "real world" in which people live, and is shaped by institutions such as family, religion, and government, as well as patterns of activity such as economic and justice systems. The Culture World is the locus for a people's language, art, values, ideologies, etiquette, and so on. In addition to the two worlds that will serve as our focusing lens, two authorities come into play: experience and reason. You will recall that experience bridges the gap between how the community imagines itself as distinct from the larger society world in which it is embedded, and the requirements and expectations that the larger society places on all its citizens. Reason helps us make sense of conflicts between the worlds, as well as determine the best way to persuade others that our ideas of how the world works makes sense.

Among the social institutions that seem to be in view in the story of the Bent-Over Woman are: the woman's physical condition in light of first-century CE notions of healthcare, her status as a slave and the socio-cultural system within which slavery is embedded, and the woman's gender, especially the social implications of female slavery and "daughterhood."

THE PHYSICAL CONDITION OF THE BENT-OVER WOMAN

Virtually all commentators on the passage understand it to be some sort of healing story, although they also acknowledge that it doesn't fit any of the typical form categories identified by biblical scholars for healing—or miracle—stories. However, the woman's physical condition is clearly important; it is what brings her to Jesus' notice, and his transformation of her physical condition serves as the catalyst for the discussion between Jesus and the synagogue leader. To add to the complexity of the story, Luke's description of her condition and her transformation are quite unusual; as I discussed in the previous chapter, for example, rather than healing or curing her, Jesus liberates her (ἀπολύω). Furthermore, the word used to describe her transformation (ἀνορθόω), as used elsewhere in the biblical tradition, points primarily to God's actions on behalf of Israel's salvation, rather than to the healing of illness or disease.

To explore the woman's physical condition I use two different theoretical lenses in this chapter. The first is a medical anthropology model developed by John J. Pilch.[1] The second is a physiognomic lens used by Mikeal C. Parsons.[2] Before turning to the consideration of the woman's condition in light of these lenses, however, it may be helpful to review how Luke describes her condition. Luke describes the woman as having had "a spirit of weakness" (πνεῦμα ἀσθενείας) for eighteen years; while we have no sense from the text of the woman's age when she encounters Jesus, there is no indication that this is a condition she has had from birth. Martha Lynn Edwards notes that ἀσθενεία is used in the Hippocratic Corpus as a general term for sickness, as well as having a more specific usage as a wasting disease.[3] This is the only time in Luke (or anywhere in the gospel corpus) that the person is described as having a "spirit" of weakness, although the term ἀσθενεία is also used by Luke to describe one of the conditions from which the women who accompany Jesus and the twelve had been healed by Jesus in Luke 8:1–3.[4]

1. Pilch, *Healing in the New Testament*.

2. Parsons, *Body and Character in Luke and Acts*. In the next chapter, I will explore one more aspect of the woman's physical condition using the theoretical lens provided by disabilities studies, to examine the literary function of the woman's physical condition as a "narrative prosthesis" in literature, as developed in Mitchell and Snyder, *Narrative Prosthesis*.

3. Edwards, "Physical Disability in the Ancient Greek World," 15–16.

4. Turid Karlsen Seim suggests that the construction in Luke 8:2 should be read

In all, Luke uses ἀσθενεία or one of its cognates eight times in the gospel and seven times in Acts, each using the connotation Edwards finds in the Hippocratic Corpus—general sickness or disease, but without any sense of uncleanness or evil attached to it.[5] This immediately sets this "exorcism" apart as something other than the norm for Luke, since in all the other healing stories involving spirit possession, the spirits are identified as either unclean or evil.[6]

In using only this connotation of "general sickness" when he uses a form of ἀσθενεία, Luke seems to be different from other New Testament authors who use the term metaphorically to indicate moral failing, or in reference to weakness in the face of power. Paul, for example, generally uses these semantic meanings of ἀσθενεία in his correspondence (see, e.g., 1 Thess 5:14; Gal 4:9; 1 Cor 1:25, 27, etc.). Among the gospel writers there appears to be mixed usage, or usage in line with Luke's application of the term. In John, for example, the term is used in three stories: in the healing of the man who had been ill for 38 years (John 5:1–9), to describe the ill persons whom the multitudes had seen Jesus working his signs on (John 6:2), and to describe Lazarus's condition in John 11; in all these instances the connotation seems to be a general sickness, rather than moral failing or powerlessness, similar to Luke's usage. In Mark and Matthew, however, ἀσθενεία is used in two ways: with this sense of general sickness (Mark 6:56; Matt 10:8, and the last judgment parable in Matt 25:31–46), but also with the connotation of weakness as moral failing that prevents persons from doing what they know they ought to do, as in the parallel stories of the Passion Week scene in Gethsemane (Mark 14:38//Matthew 26:41): "the spirit is willing but the flesh is weak (ἀσθενής)." Luke appears to have eliminated this statement from his

---

as a parallel construction, making the literal translation "spirits of evil and (spirits) of weaknesses." Seim, *Double Vision*, 41–42.

5. Here are the verses in which some form of the term is used in the gospel: Luke 4:40; 5:15; 7:10 (disputed MSS tradition), 8:2; 9:2; 10:9; and 13:11, 12. It is interesting to note that, after using it twice in the same pericope in our story, Luke doesn't use any form of ἀσθενεία again in the gospel. In Acts, some form of the term is used in Acts 4:9; 5:15, 16; 9:37; 19:12; 20:35; and 28:9.

6. I stress this point because a number of persons have argued with me that since Satan is described as the woman's captor later in the passage, this must be either an evil or unclean spirit. However, Luke seems to be very careful *not* to use this language in describing the spirit affecting the woman, therefore suggesting that he has some other intent in mind. I think this is one more item in the list of reasons this passage should be seen as different from the typical genres with which it is associated.

version of the scene at Gethsemane as he finds it in his Markan source (Luke 22:39–46//Mark 14:32–50), suggesting that he does not want his audience to have this notion of moral failing in mind when he uses the term in his gospel.[7]

It is also important to note that in the other exorcisms he describes throughout the gospel, Luke is quite specific in stating that the spirit possessing the person is either evil or unclean, which he does not do here. Instead, here he describes the impact of the spirit of weakness upon the woman: she is bent over (συγκύπτουσα) and is, literally, without the power (μὴ δυναμένη) to straighten herself fully (ἀνακύψαι εἰς τὸ παντελές).[8] Her condition—the bowing down or being bent over (συγκύπτω) —is described with a word used only here in the New Testament. However, it is used in three places in the Septuagint: it refers to the wicked being bowed down by evil in Sirach twice, while in Job it refers to a gesture of humility by someone accused of wickedness.[9] We will explore the implications of this cultural usage in more detail below when we consider the physiognomic methods of analysis. First, however, we turn to the medical anthropology model, to see what insights we can gain about the Bent-Over Woman.

Medical Anthropology

John J. Pilch is concerned with enabling twenty-first-century persons living in the United States—especially biblical scholars—to engage the healing texts in the New Testament in a way that maintains the cultural integrity of the experience of first century persons who received healing

---

7. One can argue that Luke's use of a form of ἀσθενεία in Acts 20:35 is within the range of meaning of weakness in the face of power, however. In Paul's farewell speech to the elders in Ephesus he says, "You know for yourselves that I worked with my own hands to support myself and my companions. In all this I have given you an example that by such work we must support the weak (ἀσθενούντων), remembering the words of the Lord Jesus, for he himself said, 'It is more blessed to give than to receive.'" (Acts 20:34–35). This is the only time that Luke does not use the term clearly in the context of naming persons who are ill in a general sense. However, this may be a stylistic choice because of his use of the technique of ἐθωποῖια (speech-in-character) to create an address by Paul that would ring true to Luke's audience if they were familiar with Paul's writings.

8. M. Dennis Hamm notes that ἀνακύψις is generally used in relation to salvation. Hamm, "Freeing," 33.

9. The usages are: Sir 12:11 and 19:26, and Job 9:27.

from Jesus.[10] To do so, he identifies values orientation, understanding the healthcare system, and taxonomies of healing as key elements in successfully negotiating the twenty centuries between Jesus' day and our own. Thus, disease that can be "cured" is a twenty-first century notion; illness that can be made meaningful is a first century notion, for example.[11] To create a cross-cultural model that can span the differing values orientation between the Mediterranean culture of the New Testament and our day, he uses a model developed by Florence R. Kluckhohn and Fred L. Strodtbeck, which is based on three assumptions:

> (1) There are only a limited number of common human problems for which all peoples in all places must find a solution. (2) Possible solutions are neither limitless nor random; there are three. (3) All solutions, including their variants and alternatives, are present in varying degrees within the total cultural structure of every society. Though one solution dominates, the other solutions are also available.[12]

The Kluckhohn–Strodtbeck Model proposes that there are five problems that all societies deal with: 1) the principal mode of human activity; 2) interpersonal relationships; 3) time orientation; 4) relationships of humans to nature; and 5) the view of human nature.[13] Solutions to the principal mode of human activity range from being, to being-in-becoming, to doing; contemporary Western responses would tend toward the doing end of the spectrum, while first century Mediterranean responses would fall somewhere along the being to being-in-becoming end. With interpersonal relationships, ancient Mediterranean values would be oriented toward collateral (social equals or kin) or lineal (social status) relationships, while contemporary Western values focus on the individual. With respect to time orientation, the emphasis in the first century would have been the present or the past, while today in the West we focus on the future. The fourth problem, that of humanity's relationship to nature, is solved in ancient Mediterranean culture by either being subject to, or living in harmony with nature, while in contemporary Western culture we seek to master it. The final problem, the view of human nature, would

---

10. Pilch, *Healing*, xi–xiii, and passim.

11. Ibid., 13–14. One can, of course, argue that healing as meaning-making happens in our time as well, as he does in several places.

12. Ibid., 3.

13. Ibid., 4.

be seen by Jesus' contemporaries as either a mixture of good and evil, or as evil, while in the West today we begin with the presumption that human nature is good.[14] Given these possible solutions, Pilch suggests that

> the New Testament idea of health emphasizes:
> 1. being and/or becoming (that is, states), not doing (activity)
> 2. collateral and lineal relationships, not individualism
> 3. present and past time orientation, not the future
> 4. the uncontrollable factor of nature, not its manipulation or mastery
> 5. human nature as both good and bad, not neutral or correctable.[15]

With this understanding of the differences between first and twenty-first century values orientations in place, Pilch then moves on to consider the healthcare system at work in the first century. He suggests that a good definition for "health" in the first century is that offered by the World Health Organization in our day: a "state of complete physical, mental, and social well-being and not merely the absence of disease and infirmity."[16] He further suggests that there are five elements at work in any society's healthcare system:

1. A cultural hierarchy of health values

2. How the experience of illness is conceptualized

3. How illness is responded to, based on labeling, classifying, and explaining it

4. Healing activities

5. The potential outcomes for any form of illness, up to, and including, death.[17]

Of particular importance is the role of the healer and her or his interaction with the person who is ill and the social system in which that person is embedded. The healer helps the person who is ill make sense of her or his illness by helping to interpret it in light of the culture's health

14. Ibid.

15. Ibid., 12.

16. Ibid., 24. Pilch also notes that this definition is not happily accepted by Western practitioners, since it describes health as a "state" of being.

17. Ibid., 27–28.

values, by labeling, classifying, and naming it correctly, by engaging in healing activities, and by supporting potential outcomes. By linking the person's experience of illness to her or his society's cultural understanding of illness and health, the healer engages in symbolic healing.[18]

Let us think about the Bent-Over Woman story in light of these analytical models from medical anthropology, focusing first on the set of human problems and their solutions as discussed by Pilch. Pilch has suggested that in the first century, the principal mode of human activity would be a state of being. He notes, for example, that people are blind, or deaf, or lame, or have a flow of blood that will not stop, rather than experiencing a "loss of function," as we might describe it today.[19] However, Luke does not describe the woman simply as "bent over"; he goes on to give the consequences of that bent-overness: "she was unable to straighten herself fully" (v.11b). Unlike most other healings in the gospel, here the woman's inability to function becomes a component of the encounter with Jesus;[20] after his interaction with her, "immediately she was made straight" (παραχρῆμα ἀνωρθώθη), enabling her to praise God (v.13)—an activity which she had been unable to do for eighteen years. As I will discuss below, this is not a typically gendered response, in contrast to Simon's mother-in-law, for example, who, upon being healed, also "immediately" rises up (παραχρῆμα ἀναστᾶσα) and serves Simon's guests (Luke 4:38–39).[21]

The second problem identified in the values orientation model is interpersonal relations; Pilch has suggested that the typical way of relating in the first century is collateral, with lineal (i.e., hierarchical) relationships as a secondary mode. As with the woman with the hemorrhage in Luke 8:43–48, this woman has no name, and apparently no family structure of which she is a part. She does seem to be a part of the community that participates in this particular synagogue, however, in that she appears to have come to attend the meeting with the guest teacher—although not with the intent to be healed, as was the case with the woman with the hemorrhage. However, Jesus will embed both women

18. Ibid., 32.

19. Ibid., 12. See also the discussion on 112–13.

20. One could argue that the Gerasene demoniac (Luke 8:26–39) is unable to function as well (at least within the community), in that he "wears no clothes" and lives "not in a house but among the tombs" (v. 27).

21. Pilch, *Healing*, 8.

in a kinship structure by calling them "daughter," and in the case of the Bent-Over Woman will specify that she is, without question, part of the covenant family by calling her "Daughter of Abraham." As I will discuss below in the section on slavery, naming her a daughter of Abraham is a significant transformation of her social status, since as a slave her social connections to a family or a people would not exist.

The third problem in the values orientation model is the last that seems to be operative in our story, which addresses time orientation. Pilch has suggested that the first century orientation would be to the present, or possibly to the past for those who have a lineal sense of relationships, in that what happened in the past establishes status in the present.[22] The verb that Jesus uses to describe the woman's transformation (ἀπολελυ-σαι) is a perfect form of ἀπολύω. In New Testament Greek, the perfect form of the verb indicates that an event was accomplished in the past, with results existing in the present. Jesus thus says to the woman that she was already set free (perhaps when he said the prophecy in Isaiah had been fulfilled in the Nazareth synagogue?), but that her liberation continues in the present, which accords with Pilch's time orientation. However, the verb used to describe her straightening, ἀνορθόω, alludes to the establishment of the throne of David's descendents forever, as well as other references in the Septuagint to Israel's anticipated salvation and restoration, giving the woman's experience an element of the future as well. Certainly, the companion moment when the verb is used again by Luke—in Acts 15 at the Jerusalem Conference—is still in the future, not to mention on the other side of the resurrection.

The reference to Jesus' description of what has happened to the woman is a perfect segue into the healthcare system model described above; Jesus is the one who will re-conceptualize, label, re-classify, and explain the woman's condition—not as an illness, but as a condition of bondage and captivity. By naming her condition "correctly," he stands on its head the way in which the synagogue leader, the people—and, potentially, the woman herself—understand the woman's condition. He does so by "activating the symbolic connections" to their shared mythic world[23]—the world that is established by the setting of the situation—the Sabbath day. And, as I have argued in detail above, this re-conceptualizing of the woman's condition from illness to bondage is supported by Luke

22. Ibid., 10.
23. Ibid., 32–34.

in virtually every detail of the pericope—from Jesus' direct address to the afflicted person rather than the spirit (who is not identified as either unclean or evil), to the verb of transformation, to the rationale given for "working" on the Sabbath. As I will argue in more detail in the next chapter, the woman herself seems to be a metaphor for the people's own past epic history of freedom from bondage, and their hope for freedom yet to come.

Pilch has one more set of models that may prove useful in illuminating our story: taxonomies of illness. He identifies three that he sees functioning in Luke-Acts: purity/impurity, spirit involvement, and symbolic body zones.[24] The taxonomy of purity/impurity helps us to see that Luke has constructed this story differently from the other healing stories involving a spirit; as I have argued above, there is no indication that the spirit is either unclean or evil, even though Satan is named in the pericope. Satan's function, it seems, is not designed to indicate that the woman is somehow "unclean," but rather to change her status from one who is ill to one who is enslaved.

Clearly, the story of the Bent-Over Woman fits into the taxonomy of spirit involvement. However, as I have discussed above as well as in chapter 2, it is unlike all the other spirit-involved healings in Luke: as I have just noted, it is not an evil or unclean spirit, but a spirit of weakness; Jesus does not address the spirit but the afflicted person during the encounter; the spirit is therefore not rebuked or cast out, as is the case in the other spirit-involved healings in the gospel of Luke. This taxonomy thus helps us to see that Luke apparently intends for his audience to understand something different in regards to this story, rather than to see the actions of Jesus purely as a typical exorcism.

The final taxonomy Pilch identifies in relationship to healing is the taxonomy of symbolic body zones. He identifies three symbolic zones that function in healings in the first century: heart-eyes, which affect "emotion-fused thought"; mouth-ears, affecting "self-expressive speech"; and hands-feet, affecting "purposeful action."[25] Pilch argues that all of the healings involving women in Luke (and Acts) are affected in the hands-feet zone: "All of the women healed in Luke's Gospel, then, were healed in the symbolic body zone of hands-feet, the zone of purposeful activity. According to the Luckhohn–Strodtbeck model . . . the primary value

24. Ibid., 103–12.
25. Ibid., 107.

orientation for women in ancient Mediterranean culture is purposeful activity. Illness impeded these women from pursuing their dominant cultural orientation. Healing restores them to that capacity."[26]

What Pilch misses in his observation that "the bent woman is freed from a spirit of infirmity . . . and is able to stand up straight again, suggesting yet another healing in the hands-feet zone"[27] is that what is restored is her ability to engage in self-expressive speech by praising God in the public assembly—a mouth-ears function. Unlike Simon Peter's mother-in-law, who immediately begins to serve her guests once she is restored to good health (a purposeful activity that is culturally appropriate and expected for women), the (formerly) Bent-Over Woman engages in behavior that may well be seen as culturally inappropriate for women: public speech in the synagogue.[28]

All of these insights from medical anthropology serve to heighten the unusual nature of this story in Luke. Just as we found in applying traditional historical-critical exegesis methods in chapter 2, in applying these social-scientific methods we are confronted with the inescapable conclusion that Luke seems to be intending something different with this story, given how it deviates from the norm. Let us turn now to consider the story through the lens of physiognomy, to see what insights this ancient science might give us.

Physiognomy

I turn now to Mikeal C. Parsons' exploration of physiognomic categories in Luke-Acts, to shed additional light on the woman's condition. Parsons indicates that the use of physiognomy was widespread in the ancient world, from the time of Homer through at least the third century CE. In particular, he says, "physical descriptions of characters in epic, history, drama, and fiction, as well as in medical writings, were used by writers

---

26. Ibid., 109. There are only two healings of women in Acts: the raising of Tabitha/ Dorcas from the dead in Acts 9:36–43, and the exorcism of the slave girl in Acts 16:16–24. Interestingly, this gives both Peter and Paul the opportunity to heal a woman.

27. Pilch, *Healing*, 109.

28. I will discuss this possibility in more detail in chapter 4 when I explore the Communal World Luke may be addressing. For a thorough discussion of the healing of Simon Peter's mother-in-law, see Seim, *Double Message*, 57–62.

to explain the character's actions. The physiognomic consciousness that developed permeated the Greco-Roman thought world."[29]

Parsons highlights three types of physiognomic analysis that were in use by the third century BCE: the anatomical method, the zoological method, and the ethnographic method.[30] In the anatomical method, according to Parsons, "the physiognomist looks at a facial feature (e.g., the scowl or furrowed brow) and identifies its corresponding emotion. Whenever the expression is subsequently observed on a different person, the corresponding character trait can be inferred."[31] The zoological method is based on the assumption that animals are incapable of hiding their inner moral character; therefore, if one can observe physical features in human beings that are similar to those of a given animal, then one may infer that the characteristics associated with that animal (e.g., cunning foxes, timid deer, courageous lions) are characteristics shared by the person who looks like that animal.[32]

The third method, the ethnographic method, applies the same process as the zoological method, but between races of people. The body of the Roman male citizen, for example, was considered normative: "races or ethnic groups exhibiting real or presumed deviations from that body type would be subject to denigration."[33] There was also an association between the geographical location of a people and their character, so that Hippocrates could write, for example,

> Inhabitants of a region which is mountainous, rugged, high and (not) watered, where the changes of season exhibit sharp contrasts are likely to be of big physique, with a nature well adapted for endurance and courage, and such possess not a little wildness and ferocity. The inhabitants of hollow regions that are meadowy, stifling, with more hot than cold winds, and where the water is hot, will be neither tall nor well made, but inclined to be broad, fleshy, and dark-haired; they are dark rather than fair, less subject to phlegm than to bile. Similarly, bravery and endurance are not by nature part of their character, but the imposition of law can produce them artificially.[34]

29. Parsons, *Body and Character*, 17.

30. Ibid., 22–23.

31. Ibid., 23.

32. Ibid.

33. Ibid., 25.

34. Cited ibid., 24.

These physiognomic methods were particularly useful in rhetoric, according to Parsons; he notes that the ability of an orator to make connections between the physical characteristics of the subject of a speech and that person's inner nature was a skill greatly to be desired, and quotes a lengthy passage from a speech of Cicero's against L. Calpurnius Piso Cassionius as an example. Among the connections Cicero makes between Piso's physical and inner features include:

> We were not deceived by your slavish complexion, your hairy cheeks, and your discolored teeth; it was your eyes, eyebrows, forehead, in a word, your whole countenance, which is a kind of silent speech of the mind that pushed your fellow-men into delusion.[35]

Parsons suggests that the anatomical and zoological methods are helpful in deriving deeper insight as we consider Luke and Acts. He notes that Luke uses animal metaphors in several places, for example, "you brood of vipers" (Luke 3:7), Herod "the Fox" (Luke 13:32), and Jesus' exhortation to go out as "sheep among wolves" (Luke 10:3). In the ears of an audience steeped in physiognomic ways of conceptualizing the inner character of people, these references would add another layer of interpretive power to Luke's message, according to Parsons.[36] Parsons sees Luke's use of physiognomic categories as being particularly important to the theme of the community's participation in the Abrahamic covenant. He notes, "The two characters to whom Luke assigns the titles of daughter and son of Abraham [the Bent-Over Woman and Zacchaeus] are, by physiognomic standards, inferior human beings. Yet they are children of Abraham. Despite their outward appearance, positive moral character is either revealed (in the case of the bent-over woman) or produced (in the case of Zacchaeus) through an encounter with Jesus."[37] Let us now look more closely at the Bent-Over-Woman pericope, in light of these physiognomic methods.[38]

You will recall that the word chosen by Luke to describe the woman's "bent-overness" is συγκύπτω, which, as I noted above, is used only

---

35. Cited ibid., 27.

36. Ibid. See Parsons' discussion of each of these metaphors in 67–76.

37. Ibid., 82.

38. Parsons notes, as I have done, that the story of the Bent-Over Woman has been largely ignored. See his listing of the recent work on the pericope on pp. 83–85.

here in the NT, and three times in the LXX. In one of these passages, Sirach suggests:

> A person is known by his appearance,
> And a sensible person is known when first met,
> face to face.
>
> A person's attire and hearty laughter,
> And the way he walks, shows what he is.
> (Sir 19:29–30; emphasis added)

The implication in Sirach is that one's appearance is representative of one's inner character.[39] Pseudo-Aristotle, writing at about the same time as Ben Sira suggests: "Those in whom the back is very bent with the shoulders driven into the chest are of evil disposition; this is appropriate, because the parts in front which should be visible disappear."[40] Six centuries later, the physiognomist Adamantios will agree: "He who has a hunchback and whose shoulders are bent in the direction of his breast is malicious and a sorcerer."[41] Clearly, there is a cultural understanding, over a long period of time, that bent backs are to be equated with an evil or wicked character. Furthermore, as Parsons argues, the physiognomic tractates make a connection between weak backs and weak character, and that this is specifically a gendered construction: men have strong backs and are of strong character; women are, by definition, weaker, and therefore have weaker character.[42]

In addition, as one whose physical condition is described by a word that seems to be used culturally with a connotation of wickedness, Luke's audience initially may understand the woman's physical condition as a "moral" disability, especially since her disability does not fall into the traditional biblical categories of blindness, deafness, or lameness.[43] Judith Abrams notes, "Israel is sometimes characterized metaphorically as a

---

39. Page Dubois notes a similar understanding in Aristotle's *Politics* and by Socrates in Xenophon's *Memorabilia*. See Dubois, *Slaves and other Objects*, 6 and n. 13.

40. Cited in Parsons, *Body and Character*, 85.

41. Cited in Garland, *Eye of the Beholder*, 117.

42. Parsons, *Body and Character*, 85. In the ancient literature, *free* men have strong backs; enslaved men are weak (even if they are "brawny"). See the discussion on slave bodies throughout Glancy, *Slavery in Early Christianity*, and in Harrill, *Slaves in the New Testament*, 35–57.

43. Parsons notes that Luke's use of "spirit" is also likely to suggest an inner moral problem in physiognomic terms. Parsons, *Body and Character*, 86.

person with a disability. Here, the use of one gestalt to explain another is obvious: moral disability is equated with physical disability. Israel is conceived of as a body, a person; and her immorality is symbolized by various physical disabilities."[44]

I recognize that this observation seems to contradict my insistence above that Luke is seeking to counteract the cultural understanding of evilness by his careful use of ἀσθενεία throughout the gospel. My reason for making this distinction is that in this story the Lukan Jesus rejects the view that this woman's physical disability is equated to moral disability by describing her as "bound" by Satan. Her condition is not the result of being punished for sins she has committed or for a violation of purity laws; rather she has been bound and taken captive. By shifting the terms, Jesus erases the woman's disability, and reframes her condition as that of slave; he releases her (ἀπολύω) from captivity rather than healing her of a sickness.[45] In doing so, Jesus makes real his contention in the Nazareth synagogue that his mission is to release those who are oppressed. Luke thus characterizes Jesus as a prophet whose words are backed up by deeds, and, in concert with Seim's claims, the experience of the woman in this pericope does indeed concretize the prophetic claims Jesus makes in the Nazareth story.

Parsons makes one other physiognomic observation about the Bent-Over-Woman pericope that is important to address. He comments,

> Interpreters have long wondered about the choice of [the ox and the donkey] to contrast with the bent woman. They are domestic animals, thus providing a way for Jesus to show that his opponents care more for livestock than for a fellow human, but is there any

44. Abrams, *Judaism and Disability*, 76. She also notes that, in addition to Israel being personified as an individual body that is disabled (often female), disabled individuals, for example Tobit, sometimes stand in for collective Israel. I believe that Luke is using this woman to stand in for the collective community that gathers in Jesus' name. I will discuss this possibility in much more detail in chapter 4.

45. Robert C. Tannehill offers a broad definition for ἄφεσις, "release," that includes healing. Interestingly, he doesn't discuss why Luke might have chosen to use different terms in the story of the Bent-Over Woman, simply grouping it in the several stories in which Jesus responds to the oppressed and excluded. Tannehill, *The Narrative Unity of Luke-Acts*, 1: 103–139. Parsons falls into a similar trap; he describes the woman's condition as a "physical manifestation of a satanic possession" (Parsons, *Body and Character*, 86). Both Tannehill and Parsons (along with most other commentators) seem unable to see this story as anything other than a healing story, no matter how odd or different it may be.

other point of contact? The zoological method of the physiognomic handbooks sheds some light here as well . . . To an audience familiar with [negative] characterizations [of these animals], the message of the Lukan Jesus would be clear. Not only are Jesus' opponents more willing to aid an animal than a woman, but they are also more willing to aid those animals who symbolize such negative traits as cowardice, sluggishness, stupidity, laziness, or insolence than to help a daughter of Abraham whose status is masked, not reflected, by her physical condition.[46]

While it may be the case that these physiognomic characterizations of dullness and stupidity would be in the back of Luke's audience's mind as they heard this story, I think it is much more likely, as I have argued in chapter 2, that Luke is here referencing the Deuteronomic rationale for observing the Sabbath, since among those who are to be set free to rest on the Sabbath are specifically the ox and donkey (Deut 5:14). The setting of the story on the Sabbath, the argument with the synagogue leader about what one is obligated to do on the Sabbath, in which Jesus counteracts the leader's emphasis on the Exodus rationale of creation and resting from work to challenge Jesus' actions as work, and the recasting of the woman, not as someone who is ill, but as someone who is enslaved—all suggest that Luke expects his audience to understand the ox and donkey in reference to the Sabbath commandment, rather than to negative physiognomic characteristics associated with these animals.[47] As we shall see below, physiognomic considerations actually strengthen my assertion that the issue here is slavery and liberation, rather than some sort of physical illness. Let us turn now to consider this reframing of the woman's status from ill person to slave, within the context of slavery in the early Roman Empire.

---

46. Parsons, *Body and Character*, 88–89.

47. In Luke 14:5, the healing of the man with dropsy, Luke again uses ox, and, in many manuscript variants, this is paired with "donkey" rather than "son." Again, I suggest that Luke is inviting his audience to bear in mind specifically the Deuteronomic version of the fourth commandment, not simply the Exodus version, given that this healing also takes place on the Sabbath. Furthermore, this implicit citation of Deut 5:14 is in accord with my proposal that Luke is using the literary genre of the elaborated *chreia*, in which the citation of authorities was expected. Willi Braun argues that Luke 14:1–6 is also an elaborated *chreia*; see Braun, "Use of Mediterranean Banquet Traditions in Luke 14:1–24," 43–45.

THE BENT-OVER WOMAN AS SLAVE AND WOMAN

As we have seen already, the Bent-Over Woman is an ambiguous figure. The woman's posture and her spirit of weakness add to her ambiguity. Is she ill? Or is she a slave? Her posture, as we shall see below, suggests slave; her spirit of ἀσθενεία suggests she is ill (especially given Luke's other usages of the term), although a "weak" body was thought to be indicative of a slave.[48] In declaring that she is set free, Jesus lends authority to the notion that she is enslaved, but then the synagogue leader focuses on her healing. Which is it to be? I imagine the audience holds its breath, waiting to hear how the issue and the story will resolve itself. And then we hear it: "the Lord" (ὁ κύριος) rather than "Jesus" answers the synagogue leader's challenge, and describes the woman as having been wrongly enslaved for eighteen years. Furthermore, no longer is she socially dead or "natally alienated" in Orlando Patterson's phrase,[49] cut off from the familial relationships that provide her with status and social position and identity; instead, she is a daughter—and not just any daughter, but Abraham's daughter. Just like a heroine in one of the Greco-Roman novels, she is restored to her true place in her social world by the intervention of Jesus in her life.[50]

In creating the ambiguity in this story, Luke draws on a variety of social and cultural factors with which he reasonably could expect his audience to be familiar. The medical and healthcare factors lending credence to the woman's condition as illness I have discussed above. Among those related to slavery are: the social system of slavery itself,

48. Harrill, *Slaves*, 37.

49. Patterson, *Slavery and Social Death*, 5. Patterson suggests, "Alienated from all 'rights' or claims of birth, [the slave] ceased to belong in his own right to any legitimate social order . . . Not only was the slave denied all claims on, and obligations to, his parents and living blood relations but, by extension, all such claims and obligations on his more remote ancestors and on his descendents. He was truly a genealogical isolate. Formally isolated in his social relations with those who lived, he was also culturally isolated from the social heritage of his ancestors. . . . Slaves differed from other human beings in that they were not allowed freely to integrate the experience of their ancestors into their lives, to inform their understanding of social reality with the inherited meanings of their natural forebears, or to anchor the living present in any conscious community of memory" (ibid., 5). Jesus, by his interpretation of his actions, will restore the woman's genealogical ties and therefore her participation in a "community of memory"—specifically that descended from Abraham.

50. See the discussion on Greek novels in Fitzgerald, *Slavery and the Roman Literary Imagination*, 94–98.

the literary conventions of slavery found in various types of Greco-Roman literature, and the way in which slavery is depicted in Judaism, especially in the Septuagint. He could also draw on the physiognomic approach to making judgments about the character of persons based on visible physical features. Let us turn to explore each of these factors in more detail.

Slavery was a ubiquitous feature of the ancient world. Embedded in all facets of life, slaves served to define what it meant to be a free citizen, especially in ancient Athens and throughout the Roman Empire.[51] To give a sense of what this means, Richard Horsley has identified a number of binary relationships in which elements of slavery served to support the identity of free Greek and Roman (male) citizens:[52]

TABLE 3: Slavery and Identity Formation

Free (male) Citizen	Slave (male and female)
Belonging to society	Not-belonging
Free	Not-free
Unavailable for:	Available for:
• corporal punishment	• corporal punishment
• sex	• sex
• other types of humiliation	• other types of humiliation
With Honor	Without Honor

The economic need for slaves was directly related to the need to maintain one's honor. Horsley contends that the master's honor was sustained and augmented through the ownership of slaves, which obviated the master's need to work for a living, either for himself, or in an even more degrading and shameful context, for another. Slaves not only did the work, they "also served the master's psychological need to dominate—indeed, to dominate other human beings absolutely, to the point that they were not really humans in the same sense as the master."[53]

To modern eyes, especially those familiar with American slavery, ancient slavery has often been seen as somehow different, as somehow

51. Ibid., 1–12. See also Beavis, "Ancient Slavery as an Interpretive Context," 37–54, and Dubois, *Slaves and Other Objects.*

52. Horsley, "Slave Systems of Classical Antiquity," 30. Horsley is here working with Orlando Patterson's conception of slavery as social death, reinforced by a slave's "outsider" status.

53 Ibid., 30–31.

less problematic or onerous than slavery in the United States. Ancient slavery, as opposed to American slavery, has sometimes been seen as akin to service in British aristocratic households, especially as it is romanticized in film and television, such as the famous PBS Masterpiece Theatre series, *Upstairs Downstairs*, from the 1970s.[54] Page Dubois notes that classics scholars, for example, have been reluctant to acknowledge that the seedbed of democracy and freedom, ancient Athens, was made possible because of the slaves who made it feasible for free citizens to have enough leisure to engage in public activities.[55] Mary Ann Beavis observed in a 1992 article in the *Journal of Biblical Literature* that English translators and scholars of the New Testament were reluctant to use the term "slave" in their translations and critical analyses, even though they knew that the Greek word δοῦλος, for example, inevitably refers to a slave in Greco-Roman literature.[56] In 1998, an issue of the Society of Biblical Literature's journal *Semeia* focused on slavery. It sought to take seriously the implications for New Testament scholarship of Orlando Patterson's sweeping discussion of slavery as social death, but noted with some dismay that there had been more than a decade between Patterson's work and their own, in which his insights had been largely ignored by biblical scholars.[57]

Since that issue of *Semeia* was released, however, there has been an explosion of research and writing by biblical scholars on slavery in the ancient world, and its use as a foil for the New Testament writers. Other disciplines, such as classical studies, have also begun to explore slavery as an embedded feature of ancient society, and to take seriously its role in shaping the cultural heritage of our present day. There is now, therefore, a much more comprehensive body of research on slavery in the Hellenistic and Roman period, against which we can compare and contrast Luke's description of the Bent-Over Woman, to see how he may have been evoking slavery and its various meanings in the minds of his audience.[58]

---

54. For a proposal that the Pentateuch's legal codes understand "Hebrew slaves" as indentured servants similar to British indentured servants, see Flesher, *Oxen, Women, or Citizens?*, 18–21, and 18 n. 19.

55. Dubois, *Slaves*, 6–12, passim.

56. Beavis, "Ancient Slavery," 37, 40.

57. Callahan, et al., "Introduction: The Slavery of New Testament Studies," 2.

58. For a broad range of pertinent material over time, see, for example, Flesher, *Oxen, Women, or Citizens*; Chirichigno, *Debt-Slavery in Israel and the Ancient Near East*;

J. Albert Harrill's book on slavery returns us to the physiognomic work of Pseudo-Aristotle as he explores Paul's description of himself as having a weak bodily presence. Harrill's contention is that Paul is creating an imagined persona for himself using προσωποποιία (the technique of "speech-in-character") that draws on the literary conventions of the servile flatterer.[59] In referring to Pseudo-Aristotle's discussion of how appearance reflects one's status as slave or free, Harrill notes, "The author teaches that "freedom of the soul follows freedom in the appearance of the body," which means loose-knit and agile shoulders, feet, and thighs (4.811a1–4). The servile and cowardly is the inverse of this loose and well proportioned body form, with bent body carriage constrained in movement . . . (3.80b5–12)."[60]

Harrill observes that not only literature, but material artifacts such as Attic vases bear out this understanding of the servile, bent-over physical appearance as representative of the slave body, as opposed to the upright carriage and broad shoulders of the free body.[61] While Harrill is primarily concerned about the male body, and how Paul constructs the masculinity of his assumed persona in 2 Corinthians, the ancient sources remind us why the "bent carriage" of the (male) slave was so abhorrent: because weakness was associated with being female. A female slave would thus be doubly impacted by the physiognomic equating of weakness and servile posture.[62]

In Luke's story, the Woman, who is bent over and, literally, "without the power" to straighten herself fully, may therefore have been "read" as a slave body by Luke's audience, as much as she was read as someone who was spirit-possessed and therefore "ill."[63] Reading the Bent-Over

---

Joshel and Murnaghan, eds., *Women and Slaves In Greco-Roman Culture*; Fitzgerald, *Slavery and the Roman Literary Imagination*; Glancy, *Slavery in Early Christianity*; Hezser, *Jewish Slavery in Antiquity*; Harrill, *Slaves in the New Testament*; Dubois, *Slaves and Other Objects*.

59. Harrill, *Slaves*, 19, 40.

60. Cited in Harrill, *Slaves*, 41.

61. Ibid., 37.

62. Parsons, *Body and Character*, 85.

63. Steve Mason notes that Greek and Roman audiences expected to be challenged to "complete the story for themselves so as to feel respected by the author/speaker." Luke clearly respects his audience, given the number of subtle allusions to his audience's foundational texts in this passage and throughout Luke-Acts. Mason, "Of Audience and Meaning," 50.

Woman as a "slave" actually may be strengthened by Luke's description of the spirit that binds her as one of weakness rather than one that is either unclean or evil, since a form of the same word often was used to denigrate the "weak" slave body.[64] She is depicted almost as a caricature of the stereotypical bent-over, "weak" slave posture of Greco-Roman literature; indeed, given the woman's posture, Jesus' view of her physical condition as bondage rather than illness, may have been seen by Luke's audience as somewhat unremarkable, if the "physiognomic consciousness" was as culturally embedded as Parsons and Harrill argue.[65]

Jennifer Glancy's work on slavery illuminates the ways in which a woman depicted as a slave is likely to be understood by an audience in the first or second centuries CE. Glancy reminds us that, because the slave's body was not her or his own, but instead belonged to the slave-owner, it was impossible for a slave to "maintain the integrity of the borders" of her or his body: in other words, slaves were always sexually available, to be penetrated and used by the master and the free members of the household as they saw fit.[66] Because the children of a slave woman were automatically the property of her owner, a female slave's reproductive capacity was one way to enlarge the wealth of the household without increasing the number of heirs among whom the estate would be divided upon the householder's death. Inscriptional evidence in Roman Egypt suggests that this capacity made female slaves in their prime reproductive years especially valuable.[67] Additionally, some female slaves were sold as concubines, and thus had specific "wife-like" responsibilities, but without the social protections accorded to free women.[68] Another pos-

64. Harrill, *Slaves*, 41. He notes that the association of slavishness with weakness was particularly the case in Greek and Roman drama.

65. Parsons, *Body and Character,* 85, and Harrill, *Slaves*, 48, *passim*. It is not clear whether female slaves would be depicted in a bent-over state in material goods; the issue for Harrill, especially, is the slave male body vs. the free male body, and he notes that the physiognomic tradition focuses on the male, rather than the female body. Ibid., 41. However, Parsons does cite the connection between strong /straight/male backs and weak/bent/female backs in the physiognomic texts. Parsons, *Body and Character,* 85.) See also the discussion on women's bodies and early Christianity in Braun, "Body, Character and the Problem of Femaleness in Early Christian Discourse," 108–17.

66. Glancy, *Slavery*, 21, *passim*. All the other authors I cite in this section, when addressing female slaves, make these same points.

67. Saller, "Women, Slaves, and the Economy of the Roman Household," 202.

68. Hezser, *Jewish Slavery in Antiquity,* 189–90. The classic biblical example of this reality is the story of Hagar and Sarah in Gen 16:1–16.

sible fate for a female slave was being used as a prostitute, or sold into prostitution.[69]

By specifying that the Bent-Over Woman has been bound for eighteen years, Luke's audience is likely, therefore, to presume that the woman is in, or has been in, her most sexually active, prime reproductive years during this period, the time when she was most valuable to her owner as a method for increasing his property—and most unable to control her own body.[70] Carolyn Osiek suggests that the implications of this reality meant that the female slave could "lay no claim to chastity or shame, which have no meaning" in a society grounded in a cultural system of honor/shame, and in which slaves, by definition, "are totally lacking in honor, either ascribed or attributed, in their interactions with free persons." Unlike a free woman, whose honor was based on maintaining the "sexual propriety appropriate to her state," the slave woman had no right to sexual privacy; at most what could be violated were the property rights of her owner.[71]

How would Luke's audience respond to the story of the Bent-Over Woman, assuming they did understand the woman, not as someone who was demon- or spirit-possessed and consequently "ill," but rather as a female slave whom Jesus releases from her bondwoman status? For those among his audience familiar with the Septuagint, Luke's use of ἀπολύω and daughter together might call to mind Exodus 21:7–11, which deals with the "release" (ἀπελεύσεται) of a daughter who has been sold as a (household) slave (οἰκέτις), most likely as a concubine.[72] In this passage,

---

69. Glancy, *Slavery*, 21.

70. Glancy notes that while male slaves might be manumitted at age 30, female slaves were unlikely to be manumitted prior to menopause—if they lived through the rigors of childbearing and slavery to reach that milestone. Ibid., 17.

71. Osieck, "Female Slaves, Porneia, and the Limits of Obedience," 256–57.

72. So Flesher, *Oxen, Women, Citizens*, 17 n. 17. He seems to believe that since this legislation is about concubinage, it is somehow different from the other Pentateuchal passages dealing with Hebrew slaves, and that being a concubine is not precisely the same thing as being a slave. He further contends that the Pentateuch understands "Hebrew slaves" as indentured (male) servants, rather than as chattel slaves. He argues that the Hebrew slave is never forced to give up his (*sic*) identity as an Israelite, or to give up his social status or ability to inherit, and therefore is not to be understood as property in the same way as (non-Hebrew) chattel slaves. Furthermore, Flesher does not appear to be convinced that the Pentateuchal legislation pays particular attention to female slaves, simply lumping them together with male slaves, as in Deuteronomy 15. See his complete discussion of "the Concept of Slavery in Scripture," in ibid., 11–26.

the father is instructed not to seek her release in the seventh year, as is to happen with male slaves. Instead, she is to remain with her "master" (κύριος) as his "wife" (concubine), unless the master: a) chooses to let her be redeemed because she "displeases" him; or b) gives the woman to his son as the son's betrothed, in which case the master is to treat her as a daughter. If the master keeps her for himself, but then takes another wife as well, he is required not to diminish her upkeep or conjugal rights. If he fails in any of these responsibilities, the woman is to "go out" free, without having to repay her purchase price. Above all, she is not to be sold to a "foreign" master, that is, someone outside Israel; rather she is to be redeemed (presumably by her father or his kin). In this way, while the young woman's bodily boundaries may have been violated, Israel's boundaries will remain intact, in keeping with scripture's view that Israelites should have no other master but God. Catherine Hezser sees a practical motive behind this difference between the treatment of male and female Hebrew slaves in the Exodus text: "The reason for this regulation probably was that the girl, even if freed, would hardly have found a marriage partner and subsistence, since she was commonly suspected of having had sexual intercourse with her master. If she remained a member of the master's household and in good standing, she would be better off, since she would at least receive food and clothes."[73]

The nexus of ἀπολύω, κύριος, and daughter (θυγάτηρ) in both the Exodus passage and the Bent-Over-Woman story may well have created a linkage between the two passages in the mind of Luke's audience, especially since the Exodus passage follows the recounting of the Ten Commandments in Exodus 20. However, Jesus does exactly the opposite of the instructions to the father in Exod 21:7; he "sets free" the daughter, restoring her to her ancestral family, the family of Abraham, apparently without worrying about whether any of the stipulations in the Exodus passage under which the woman was allowed to be redeemed were in effect. Instead, he follows the provisions of Deuteronomy 15:12–18, in which female and male slaves are to be treated in the same way, by being released in the seventh year. In doing so, Luke also suggests the pos-

---

73. Hezser, *Jewish Slavery in Antiquity*, 189. However, the scriptures include the troubling story of the Levite's concubine in Judges 19, in which the concubine is sent out to be raped by the men of Gibeah, who wanted to engage in intercourse with the Levite. His honor is maintained at the cost of the woman's life, emphasizing that she is still a slave and subject to her owner's will, even if she is a concubine.

sibility that the woman is a debt-slave, since both the Exodus 21 and the Deuteronomy 15 passages deal specifically with the release of persons from debt-slavery during the Sabbatical Year. Walter Brueggemann has suggested that Luke has intentionally made the connection between the release of slaves and forgiveness of debts throughout his gospel, as a sign of the Jubilee that Jesus announces in Nazareth. He observes, "in the ancient world (even as now) the primary reason for prison was to contain poor people who are locked up for indebtedness. Cancellation of debts permits reentry into public life with dignity and freedom. The Jubilee Year is the intervention of God, who breaks the vicious cycle—indebtedness and poverty—which is kept going by inhumane practices of land, taxes, and debts . . . Jesus, and *especially* Jesus in Luke, is implementing the Jubilee Year."[74]

There is yet another literary convention related to female slaves that seems to be in play in Luke's story of the Bent-Over Woman, and which has ties to Brueggemann's proposal about Luke's use of the Jubilee theme. Glancy notes that a feature of the non-scriptural literature contemporary to Luke-Acts in which female slaves are present as characters, such as the Greco-Roman romances, includes a theme of mistaken identity, in which a freeborn woman is kidnapped or otherwise mistaken for a slave, and only through a series of unlikely occurrences is able to maintain her honor—in other words, her sexual integrity.[75] It is possible to imagine that Luke had this literature in mind as he depicted Jesus as "the Lord" setting the woman free and naming her as "daughter of Abraham." In doing so, he re-establishes her kinship connections, so that she is no longer "natally alienated." Instead, she experiences the effects of the Jubilee and Sabbatical Years, as she goes out free from her period of bondage, restored to her rightful place in the covenant family.

---

74. Brueggemann, "Restlessness and Greed," 103–5; emphasis added. As I argued in chapter 2, there seems to be a literary relationship among the Bent-Over Woman, the Woman who Anoints Jesus, and the Lord's Prayer in such a way that the expectations of Deuteronomy 15 (and consequently the Jubilee Year) are met parabolically in the experiences of these two women. For a thorough and very detailed analysis of the three sets of manumission laws I touch on in this chapter (Exod 21:7–11; Deut 15:12–18; and Lev 25:1—26:13) and their relationship to one another, see Chirichigno, *Debt-Slavery in Israel*, especially 344–57.

75. Glancy, *Slavery*, 52–53. See also the very helpful discussion of the differences and commonalities among the ideal and satirical Greek novels and Jewish novels in Wills, "Depiction of Slavery in the Ancient Novel," 113–32.

Indeed, she quite literally experiences the promise God makes to Israel if they follow obediently the statutes and ordinances God lays out for the Jubilee. Leviticus 26:13 says: "I am the Lord your God who brought you out of the land of Egypt, to be their slaves no more; I have broken the bonds (τὸν δεσμὸν) of your yoke and made you walk erect." In Luke's story, Jesus (the Lord) performs the actions of God, enabling the woman to walk erect by releasing her from the bond (ὁ δεσμός) that had prevented her from walking erect for eighteen years (Luke 13:16). In doing so, Jesus brings to concrete fruition the Jubilee expectations—the year of God's favor—that he laid claim to as part of his inaugural sermon in the Nazareth synagogue (Luke 4:16–21). Moreover, an unspoken portion of the verse he quotes from Isaiah 58:6 in that scene uses the Jubilee image of "loosing (λυε) the 'bindings' (σύνδεσμον) of injustice/undoing the thongs of the yoke" (Isa 58:6ab), language that is echoed in Luke 13:16: "[ought not this woman] be loosed from this bond (λυθῆναι ἀπὸ τοῦ δεσμοῦ) [on the day of the Sabbath]?" Given that the Isaiah passage concludes with a description of the proper observation of the Sabbath (Isa 58:13–14), Luke's layering of Jubilee images in the story of the Bent-Over Woman suggests that she should be thought of in connection with Jesus' statement that the Jubilee prophecy of Isaiah is fulfilled *today* (Luke 4:21).

THE BENT-OVER WOMAN AS DAUGHTER OF ABRAHAM

The final element of Luke's Society World we will explore in this chapter is Jesus' description of the woman as a "daughter of Abraham." The phrase is used only here in the New Testament, and, as Turid Karlsen Seim argues, seems to be original to Luke, if not unique, since there are a few references in the rabbinic literature (presumably later than Luke) to "daughters of Abraham."[76] As I mentioned above, the closest near use of the term in biblical literature is in 4 Maccabees, when the mother of the seven martyred sons is described as being a "daughter of the god-fearing strength of Abraham" (4 Macc 15:28). This strength is manifested as she steadfastly uses reason to overcome her grief at the torture and death of all seven of her sons—in order to be true to the commandment of God. Seim notes a distinction between the martyred mother and the

---

76 Seim, *Double Message*, 43–47. Seim notes that the Talmudic references seem to be equating Daughters of Abraham with "respectable" Jewish women. Ibid., 47.

Bent-Over Woman: the martyred mother shows that she has the attributes of faithful piety that Abraham shows in the sacrifice of Isaac (Gen 22), and so therefore seems to be following the example or model of Abraham. In Luke 13:16, however, the woman is described as a daughter of Abraham simply as "an observation of fact"[77]—rather than because she has accomplished some great act of piety or faithfulness. Seim remarks,

> The surprising element is not primarily the fact that a Jewish woman is called Abraham's daughter. Abraham normally had sons, but daughters could exist too. The surprising element is rather that the woman about whom this is said is not a paragon of piety, but a woman who has been possessed for a great part of her life. She is not given any attributes that might legitimate a special likeness or relationship to Abraham. Abraham thus plays no role as model or typological prototype. A possessed woman is quite simply confirmed as Abraham's daughter. She is included without conditions in Abraham's family.[78]

If, however, one considers the possibility that Luke is portraying the woman, not as possessed, but rather as someone who is enslaved, then naming the woman as "daughter of Abraham" is not simply an observation of fact; it is, instead, claiming her as an acknowledged, legitimate descendent, with all the rights inherent in that status. To name her as a daughter of Abraham, if one understands her as having been enslaved, is to restore all the ties that had to have been severed in order to make someone "socially dead," and therefore a slave.[79]

It is also hard to escape the linkage between the description of the Bent-Over Woman as a daughter of Abraham, and the preaching of John the Baptist prior to the baptism of Jesus (Luke 3:7–9), in which John says that God can raise up (ἐγεῖραι) "children of Abraham" from stones. Clearly the entire pericope surrounding John's ministry in Luke 3:1–18 is important to Luke, since in the redaction of his sources he has gone far beyond the simple weaving together of the material from Mark and Q done by Matthew to incorporate new material. Luke's unique addition to the story of John the Baptist is his preaching to the crowds (including

77. Ibid., 48. Seim also notes the rather striking lack of any reference to the Sacrifice of Isaac in Luke.

78. Ibid., 48.

79. See n. 49 above for Patterson's description of making someone a slave through the severing of social ties and relationships.

the tax collectors and the soldiers); this message will be concretized in Jesus' interaction with Zacchaeus (Luke 19:1–10), during which Jesus calls Zacchaeus "Son of Abraham" (Luke 19:9) after Zacchaeus promises to give half of his goods to the poor and restore fourfold anything of which he has defrauded others—thus making real the Baptist's injunction in Luke 3:13 to collect no more than what is allotted. And, continuing the quotation from Isaiah found in Mark, Luke has John also say, "Every valley shall be filled, and every mountain and hill shall be made low, and the crooked shall be made straight, and the rough ways made smooth; and all flesh shall see the salvation of God" (Luke 3:5–6). Luke is likely making a connection to the themes raised in Mary's song that the lowly shall be raised up, and the mighty shall fall (Luke 1:52), and in Simeon's prediction at the dedication of Jesus in the temple that Jesus "is destined for the falling and the rising of many in Israel, and to be a sign that will be opposed so that the inner thoughts of many will be revealed" (Luke 2:34–35).[80] Furthermore, both Mary's and Zechariah's songs include the theme that God's promises made to Abraham and his descendents will be fulfilled in Mary's child (Luke 1:54–55 and Luke 1:72–75, respectively). The woman's release from bondage, enabling her to straighten up and walk erect for the first time in eighteen years, makes her the literal embodiment of these predictions, and also assures that Jesus fulfills his prophesied role.[81] Luke has thus included two scenes later in his gospel about a daughter and a son of Abraham, in which his unique additions to the story of John the Baptist (Luke 3:5–6, 10–14) are concretized through the actions and words of Jesus, linked by the Q component that "God can raise up children of Abraham from these stones" (Luke 3:8).

There is another possibility that may be in play with Luke's usage of the phrase, "daughter of Abraham." In the Septuagint, there are more than 500 verses in which "daughter" or "daughters" is used. These usages seem to cluster into five categories:

---

80. For a thorough treatment of the rising and falling theme in Luke and Acts, especially as it relates to women and men, see Arlandson, *Women, Class, and Society in Early Christianity*. In particular, see his discussion of the Bent-Over Woman, pp.168–72.

81. See the discussion on this issue in Seim, *Double Message*, 49–55, and in Hamm, "Freeing," 34–35.

1. As a generic term for female descendents (e.g. the genealogical lists in Gen 5:1–31 and Gen 11:10–25);

2. In relation to specific female children (e.g., Lot's daughters, Laban's daughters, Zelophehad's daughters, etc.);

3. As a category of persons in the legal codes (e.g., Ex 21:7 or Lev 18:10);

4. As an identifier either for the kings of Israel, who are described as X, the son of Y, the daughter of Z, or their wives, who are described as A the daughter of B;

5. As a metaphor, either for Israel, Judea, or Jerusalem (e.g. daughter of Zion, daughter of Jerusalem), or for the nations around them (e.g., daughter of Moab, daughter of Tyre, daughter of Babylon, etc.)

Clearly categories 2 and 3 are in play in this text; this particular woman is identified specifically as a daughter of Abraham, while the setting of the text calls to mind various legal codes (e.g., the command to keep Sabbath rest and Exod 21:7–11) in which "daughter" figures as a party to the legal requirement explained in the code. I would argue further, however, that she can be included in category 5 as well, a metaphor for Luke's social group. This view is in contrast to Seim, who, as I have mentioned above, argues that such a metaphorical reading "overlooks the value of the narrative in Luke 13.10–17 as a concretisation [of Jesus' proclamation of liberation in Nazareth]."[82] In looking through the lens of the Social Imagination model, however, that very concretization makes it possible to see her metaphorically. As Burton Mack has suggested, "In myths, the concentration of an unlikely combination of features in a single figure can bring thought to focus squarely on a particular, perhaps heretofore unexplored, configuration of social forces."[83] As I have sought to show in both this chapter and the previous one, Luke's story of the Bent-Over Woman concentrates an extraordinary number of unlikely features on the single figure of the woman. Surely, Luke must have had more in mind than merely showing that Jesus' words in Nazareth could come true in the lives of the people he encountered; all of the healings and teachings available to Luke in Mark and Q could have shown that

---

82. Seim, *Double Message,* 42, 54. See also the argument for understanding the woman symbolically in Hamm, "Freeing," 35, passim.

83. Mack, *Myth and the Christian Nation,* 77.

adequately. Instead, Luke chooses to add this new story, with all the various ways in which Jesus' words and deeds are elaborated and extended by the language used to describe the woman, as well as Jesus' interactions with her and with the synagogue leader. Surely, it is difficult for the audience to escape the conclusion that something different is going on here. It seems to me that the only way it is possible to understand the nature of that "something different" is to understand her in some metaphoric or symbolic way. It is to the exploration of how Luke may have intended her to be understood metaphorically, that I now turn to in chapter 4.

4

Words Made Flesh

The Bent-Over Woman as Metaphor in the Communal World of Luke-Acts

INTRODUCTION

IN THIS CHAPTER, I focus on the Bent-Over Woman as a metaphor for Luke's (ideal) community. To do so I explore the story using insights from Victor Turner's work on liminality, as well as the discipline of disabilities studies. I also return to the question of slavery in Greco-Roman and Jewish literature, this time as it is used metaphorically for a variety of purposes. In addition, I consider the implications of Luke's identification of the woman's slave-owner as Satan, building on Elaine Pagels's finding that Satan seems to be used in intra-group Jewish identity struggles to depict a connotation of "us vs. them," rather than to "demonize" Roman imperial power.

The emphasis in this chapter is thus on the Communal World of the Social Imagination model as a lens for examining the text. The reader will remember that the Communal World is the world of the group under consideration, particularly as it identifies itself as somehow separate from the larger society of which it is a part. It is shaped by its belief system and practices, as well as by the way in which it understands itself in relationship to the Mythic World. The authority of tradition—the way in which the ideals of the mythic world are "operationalized" in the life of the community, as well as the history of interpretation of those ideals over time, links these two worlds. The Communal World is linked to the Society World through the authority of experience, which embodies how the social group navigates the differences between itself and the larger society in which it is embedded.

THE BENT-OVER WOMAN AS STAND-IN
FOR LUKE'S SOCIAL GROUP

In the previous chapter, I proposed that Luke is using the Bent-Over Woman metaphorically to describe his (idealized) community. How might the Bent-Over Woman be serving as a "stand-in" for this social group? Mary Douglas has suggested, "The Body is a model which can stand for any bounded system. Its boundaries can represent any boundaries which are threatened or precarious. The body is a complex structure. The functions of its different parts and their relation afford a source of symbols for other complex structures . . ."[1] As I have argued in the previous two chapters, Luke has concentrated an extraordinary number of unusual features in the story of the Bent-Over Woman, most of which are focused in some way on the woman's body. Many of them are allusions to Israel as a collective, which suggests the possibility that Luke has constructed the woman's story so that her body can serve as a symbol of his society, as Mary Douglas has proposed above. At the very least, as Burton Mack has suggested, these features "bring thought to focus squarely on a particular, perhaps heretofore unexplored, configuration of social forces."[2] Given the number of these unlikely features, and that they all seem plausibly to be located in various elements of the imaginative world of Luke's likely audience, it seems inescapable that these unusual features are designed by Luke to function in some sort of symbolic or metaphorical way.

Before proceeding to identify additional "unlikely features" that the lens of the Communal World brings to our attention, it will be helpful to have in mind some understanding of what a metaphor is. Aristotle's theory of metaphor is useful when considering whether Luke has constructed the Bent-Over Woman metaphorically. Arthur Kirby has identified some key features of Aristotle's theory that are relevant for our discussion of the Bent-Over Woman as metaphor for Luke.[3] He suggests that metaphor:

---

1. Douglas, *Purity and Danger*, 115.

2. Mack, *Myth and the Christian Nation*, 77.

3. See Kirby's complete exploration of metaphor in Aristotle's *Poetics* and *On Rhetoric*, in Kirby, "Aristotle on Metaphor," 517–54.

1. Involves a cognitive process of decoding on the part of the audience

2. Should add sophistication to the discourse, resulting in pleasure on the part of the audience

3. Should be suited or appropriate to its context

4. Is resorted to when a thing can be named in no other way

5. Gives evidence of genius when crafted felicitously.[4]

The use of metaphors was an expected practice according to the rhetorical handbooks. For example, Theon includes metaphor as one of the devices used in developing a *chreia*, as well as in practicing paraphrasing.[5] Given that Luke appears to be well trained in the art of rhetoric, it is not surprising that he should employ metaphor in his writing. Furthermore, assuming that one does see the Bent-Over Woman functioning metaphorically, she brings a level of sophistication to Luke's discourse that is quite unlike the kingdom parables that follow immediately upon her story; these parables answer the question, "What is the Kingdom of God like?" with familiar daily activities and experiences.[6] In contrast, to understand the Woman's story fully requires a thorough knowledge of the scriptures (i.e., Septuagint) and an appreciation of allusion in support of rhetorical argumentation.

How does the "cognitive process of decoding" metaphor take place in the interaction between the text and the reader? Karin Adams suggests, in her exploration of the use of metaphor in Hosea 4:13–14, that metaphor is more than simply a comparison between two things without using either "like" or "as."[7] Using Max Black's work on metaphor, she contends that metaphor is instead an interaction that "brings together two fundamentally *dissimilar* things in a purposeful way *to create meaning*."[8] Furthermore, the author and the audience participate together in the meaning-making; in order for a metaphor to be successful, the author needs the audience to understand the "associated commonplaces" he or

---

4. Adapted from ibid., 547.

5. Kennedy, *Progymnasmata*, 18, 70.

6. The answers are: a grain of mustard seed (Luke 13:18–19) and leaven in 3 measures of flour (Luke 13:20–21).

7. Adams, "Metaphor and Dissonance," 295.

8. Ibid., 296 (emphasis in original).

she is playing off, related to the thing serving as the metaphorical vehicle. If the audience does not understand them, then the metaphor will fail in its rhetorical purpose.[9]

If we apply this understanding of metaphor to the Bent-Over Woman, we immediately see some of the dissonances that are at play in Luke's presentation of her. At the surface level, we see a crippled woman who is healed by Jesus and is thus able to stand up straight, similar to the paralyzed man who is lowered down through the roof and is able to take up his bed and walk, his sins having been forgiven (Luke 5:17–26). As I argued in the previous two chapters, however, Jesus neither forgives her sins nor heals her; rather, he "sets her free." She is raised up, not in the usual way but with language used to describe the restoration of the throne of David. She is depicted through Jesus' language, not as an ill person but rather as a slave who is released in keeping with the Sabbatical Year traditions, and who literally, as a daughter of Abraham, embodies the fulfillment of God's promise to Israel that those released in the Jubilee Year will be able to walk erect. Furthermore, the dispute between Jesus and the synagogue leader is not about what is lawful to do on the Sabbath, but rather about what one is obligated to do. In all these ways, the woman is presented differently from the typical Sabbath controversy/healing/miracle/exorcism stories with which Luke's audience may be familiar from other sources, as well as Luke's use of them elsewhere in his gospel. But what meaning does Luke hope will be created through this dissonance? I would argue that he anticipates that the dissonance will catch the attention of his audience in such a way that they will be encouraged to see the woman metaphorically as a representation of themselves as the community that gathers in Jesus' name.

Dennis Hamm has argued that, in addition to the use of ἀνορθόω with its connection to the restoration and salvation of Israel in the Septuagint (and its apparent similar usage in Acts 15:16–18), there are five additional considerations that suggest that Luke understands the woman as the metaphorical embodiment of the (new/true) Israel, the community that gathers in Jesus' name:

9. Ibid., 296–97.

1. The use of the phrase "daughter of Abraham" by rabbinic sources as a name for the entire community.

2. The parable of the mustard seed, which immediately follows the story of the Bent-Over Woman alludes to Ezekiel 17:23, "where the tree hosting the birds is an image of Israel restored."

3. The image of persons coming from the four directions in order to participate in the banquet of Abraham (Luke 13:28–29) is also one of Israel restored.

4. The likelihood that the portrait of the Jerusalem Community in Acts is to be seen as the fulfillment of the end-time restoration of Israel.

5. A connection between the story of the Bent-Over Woman in Luke and the Man Born Lame in Acts 3:1–10, where the healing of the man can be seen as the "symbolic acting out" of the Christian community as Israel restored.[10]

Thus, in seeing the Woman within the intertextuality of her literary surroundings, there are additional "itineraries of meaning," in Paul Ricoeur's phrase,[11] that suggest that Luke is, indeed, expecting his audience to understand her metaphorically as a depiction of themselves.

THE BENT-OVER WOMAN AS LIMINALITY PERSONIFIED

The ability of the woman to be understood metaphorically is further strengthened by the liminality of the story. Victor Turner notes, "Liminal entities are neither here nor there; they are betwixt and between the positions assigned and arrayed by law, custom, convention, and ceremonial."[12] Such entities can therefore be imbued with a variety of meanings, since they are not fixed in any given social structure.

Turner goes on to suggest that the liminality of persons disrupts traditional social structures, and identifies two different models of "human interrelatedness" that can be affected by this disruption. Society

---

10. Hamm, "Freeing," 35. Several of these considerations are based on Hamm's analysis of the Bent-Over Woman pericope functioning as the central moment within a chiastic literary structure that spans Luke 12:49—13:35. See his discussion in ibid., 29–31.

11. Ricoeur, "Bible and Imagination," 146.

12. Turner, "Liminality and Communitas," 95.

in the first model is highly structured and differentiated, usually with what he calls a "hierarchical politico-legal-economic system" in which persons are separated by categories of "more or less." The second model emerges during the liminal period, and is "an unstructured, or rudimentarily structured and relatively undifferentiated comitatus, community, or even communion of equal individuals who submit together to the general authority of the ritual elders." Turner goes on to say, "I prefer the Latin term "*communitas*" to "community," to distinguish this modality of social relationship from an "area of common living."[13] Adding to this notion of liminality in social structures, David T. Mitchell and Sharon L. Snyder suggest that using literary characters that are disabled enables authors to "play" with "macro [social] and micro [individual] registers of meaning-making," which they further suggest gives the body a "liminal" role in the representational process of literature.[14]

Given these understandings of how liminality functions in both social systems and literature, let me suggest that the Bent-Over-Woman story is designed by Luke to provide a narrative space that is "betwixt and between" so that his audience can imagine—or perhaps, understand—their social relationships as a sustained "*communitas*" of equal individuals.[15] Luke has, in fact, embedded the woman in a story that is rife with many types of liminality:

1. ***Liminality of geography:*** The encounter with Jesus takes place while he is somewhere "on the way" from Galilee to Jerusalem, part of Luke's "greater interpolation" betwixt and between these two geographical poles of the narrative structure of his Markan source

2. ***Liminality of time:*** The encounter with Jesus takes place on the Sabbath, a "threshold" day in which the regular activities of life are set aside, and in which hierarchical social distinctions are set aside

---

13. Ibid., 96 (italics in original).

14. Mitchell and Snyder, *Narrative Prosthesis*, 62. See the use of "social" for macro and "individual" for micro in Mitchell's somewhat shortened and revised version of this discussion: Mitchell, "Narrative Prosthesis and the Materiality of Metaphor," in Brueggemann, et al., eds., *Disability Studies,* 27. See also the section on "The Materiality of Metaphor," 24–29.

15. This is in fact the type of social formation Luke will depict in Acts as he describes the post-Pentecost community of believers (Acts 2:43–47, 4:32–35).

as well, so that all of creation may experience the rest that God experienced, and the liberation from bondage that Israel experienced.[16]

3. *Liminality of place:* The encounter takes place in the synagogue, which is a gathering in which the community comes together to discuss issues and concerns outside the normal course of daily events. Further, this is Jesus' final visit to a synagogue in Luke's gospel, in which the words spoken in his first narrated visit (Luke 4) become flesh in the encounter with the woman.

4. *Liminality of social status:* The woman enters the narrative as a disabled person, becomes a slave, and ends as a "daughter of Abraham."

5. *Liminality of action:* This is the only Sabbath controversy in the gospel which addresses what one is obligated to do on the Sabbath, rather than what is lawful.

6. *Liminality of person:* This is the only Sabbath controversy surrounding a woman.

When combined with the "liminality" of her disability, which is not a typical disability in the biblical literature, these liminal features provide abundant room for the audience's imagination to play in alternative social formations. As an example, let us focus for a moment on the liminalities of person and place and imagine what possibilities the story might engender in the audience's mind.

Since the woman "appears" while Jesus is teaching, it is possible to assume that Luke intends for his audience to imagine her at the outer edge of the gathering when Jesus first sees her. In calling her to himself, Jesus physically brings her from the margins of the social group to its center; in bringing her "front and center" he eliminates any possibility that she can stay hidden or invisible—she is no longer "out of sight/out of mind." Jesus calls her to him using the same verb (προσφωνέω) he used to call the disciples to himself prior to choosing the twelve apostles in Luke 6:12–16, a change Luke makes to his Markan source for this episode. Mark uses the verb προσκαλέομαι, which Matthew retains.[17]

---

16. See Walter Brueggemann's discussion of Sabbath in his essay, "Restlessness and Greed," 79–110.

17. Luke adds the verb προσφωνέω to Pilate's address to the crowds (where ἀπολύω is also used). It is also found in both Matthew and Luke's versions of the peri-

One can therefore imagine that his audience may well understand her as a disciple. Just a few pericopae earlier, of course, Jesus has affirmed Mary's choice to sit and listen—thereby obeying the imperative of the voice from the cloud at Jesus' transfiguration (Luke 9:35)—over Martha's choice to fulfill the role society expects of her as hostess (Luke 10:38–42). By having Mary follow the instruction to listen while Jesus affirms her choice, however, Luke draws attention to Mary's actions, which fall in the symbolic body zone of mouth-ears. Martha's, on the other hand, are focused in the symbolic body zone of hands-feet, or purposeful action. Thus Mary and Martha's actions seem to be opposed to each other in much the same way that the result of the Bent-Over Woman's "healing" is opposed to the result of the healing of Simon's mother-in-law.[18]

What is significant here in the story of the Bent-Over Woman is that this woman's discipleship is affirmed by Jesus in the public space of the synagogue, rather than in the private space of the home.[19] Luke portrays the (formerly) Bent-Over Woman's actions in language similar to that with which the author of 1 Timothy describes the appropriate behavior of the men who participate in the public life of his community (1 Tim 2:8): once she is liberated from her bondage, not only does she stand up straight, she praises God—presumably aloud, in the center of the public gathering, which obviously includes men.[20] If she is designed

---

cope from Q related to wisdom's "children" (Luke's term; they are wisdom's "deeds" in Matthew).

18. Mary Rose D'Angelo has suggested that Luke is delegitimizing Martha's "active" discipleship by affirming Mary's "passive" discipleship. See her discussion, as well as additional scholarship related to this notion in D'Angelo, "Women in Luke-Acts," 453–55, passim. Using Pilch's taxonomy of symbolic body zones, however, I would argue that Luke is subtly promoting women's full discipleship through Jesus' affirmation of Mary's behavior; Pilch, *Healing*, 107.

19. In describing the synagogue as a "public space," I am not offering any conclusions about whether synagogues existed as physical buildings in the first century CE, rather that the people came together in a public location to engage in the activities of the synagogue. See McKay, *Sabbath and Synagogue*, 5–6, passim. The woman's praise of God in the public space of the synagogue is also in contrast to Jesus' mother Mary's song, which is sung apparently only to Elizabeth, presumably in the private space of Elizabeth's home. For an analysis of women's participation in the synagogue, see Brooten, *Women Leaders*.

20. The author of 1Tim 2:11–12 enjoins women to keep silent, especially in the presence of men. Men, on the other hand, pray in every place, "lifting up holy hands without anger or argument" (1Tim 2:8). For a further discussion of the differences between these two texts in light of Pierre Bourdieu's analysis of the control of women's posture as

by Luke to be representative of the social group that gathers in Jesus'
name, then one could assume that he imagines that women are expected
to participate as disciples, not just in the domestic space of the home, but
also fully in the public gathering of the community. This possibility gains
credence as we see the inclusion of women in the post-Pentecost community in Jerusalem on an equal footing with men in Acts 5:14, where
Luke reports that "multitudes both of men and women" (πλήθη ἀνδρῶν
τε καὶ γυναικῶν) are add to the believers in the Lord.[21]

Let me pause here to consider some of the scholarly work that has
been done on Luke's depiction of women as disciples in both Luke and
Acts, to see how my analysis of the Bent-Over Woman as a metaphor
for discipleship might be received. Robert J. Karris, in his Presidential
Address to the Catholic Biblical Association of America in 1993, described the issue of women's role in the community as a "storm center" in Lukan studies, heightened by feminist scholarship moving into
a secondary phase of more critical analysis of the texts.[22] Through his
analysis of several Lukan texts, he came to the conclusion that Luke is
clearly including women among the disciples of Jesus (e.g., Luke 8:1–3;
22:14–38; 23:49, 55–56).[23]

Mary Rose D'Angelo, on the other hand, has proposed that as part
of his goal "to demonstrate the 'surety' (ἀσφάλεια) of the Christian
message" to Theophilus (Luke 1:3), Luke is also concerned to show "its
safety, that is, the community's ability to live with the empire. The ap-
pearances of women in Luke-Acts must also conform to the surety
of the Christian instruction . . ."[24] D'Angelo claims that Luke is thus
seeking to show to the world at large that women within the Christian
community are controlled in ways that are acceptable to conventional

---

symbolic power in 1960s Algeria, see Houghtby-Haddon, "Body as Subject." One might
also compare this depiction to the disputed Pauline passage in 1 Cor 14:34, which parallels 1 Tim 2:11–12.

21. See Robert C. Tannehill's discussion of women as disciples in Luke in *Narrative
Unity*, 1:132–39.

22. Karris, "Women and Discipleship," 1–19. He also includes summaries of the
scholarship on both sides of the Luke as positive vs. negative toward women divide in
his notes. See especially notes 2, 4, and 7.

23. Ibid., 11. Not too surprisingly, the Bent-Over Woman was not included in his
analysis.

24. D'Angelo, "Women and Discipleship," 448.

social mores, rather than engaging in activities that could be seen as disruptive to the social order.[25]

In a similar vein to D'Angelo, Willi Braun has suggested that neither Luke nor other "women-friendly" Christian texts are women-friendly in reality. He observes: "In all early Christian discourses the problem with women is that they are female . . . [O]n the whole, the evidence in early Christian texts overwhelmingly insinuates that the overarching Christian rallying cry on issues of gender and femaleness was something like: 'Flee from the madness and the bondage of femininity, and choose for yourselves the salvation of masculinity' . . . Furthermore, all the major types of early Christian solutions to the 'female problem' arguably proceed from that rallying cry."[26] Braun further suggests that "the 'totality' of Graeco-Roman culture was univocal: humans with female bodies represented humans of deficient personhood" which led to "Christian and other women's desire to achieve manliness of piety and character . . ."[27]

Mary Ann Beavis takes a different view, however, in her critical examination of scholarship challenging the possibility of gender egalitarianism in early Christianity. In particular, she notes that there is "a substantial body of ancient literature that can be described as 'utopian' in that it posits ideal societies either as theoretical possibilities, as existing in remote parts of the world, in the past, or in the future. Some of these works envision egalitarian social arrangements as part of the utopian ideal."[28] In addition, she suggests that ancient authors' ability to write about such ideal societies indicates that it was possible both to imagine alternative social arrangements and to implement them, even if there was "not a perfectly realized social reality conforming to modern feminist ideals, but real efforts of women and men to coexist as equals, under a variety of conditions and understandings of the reign of God."[29]

---

25. Ibid., 442–43.

26. Braun, "Body, Character, and the Problem of Femaleness," 109, 111. One immediately thinks of Logion 114 in the *Gospel of Thomas*: "Simon Peter said to them, 'Make Mary leave us, for females don't deserve life.' Jesus said, 'Look, I will guide her to make her male, so that she too may become a living spirit resembling you males. For every female who makes herself male will enter the kingdom of Heaven.'" "The Gospel of Thomas," in Miller, ed., *The Complete Gospels*, 322.

27. Braun, "Body, Character, and the Problem of Femaleness," 115.

28. Beavis, "Christian Origins, Egalitarianism, and Utopia," 44.

29. Ibid., 48–49.

The reader will not be surprised to learn that I find the analyses of Karris and Beavis more in line with my analysis of Luke's purposes as they are displayed in the story of the Bent-Over Woman. Given Luke's language in this pericope, it seems inescapable to me that he intends her to be seen as a disciple, and potentially as more than that—as the embodiment of the (liminal) egalitarian "*communitas*" (to use Turner's terminology) of disciples that gathers in Jesus' name. Further, it seems that he identifies this *communitas* with the "true" Israel that experiences the fulfillment of God's promise that the reestablishment of the throne of David's descendents will come to pass, although perhaps in an unexpected way. Let us turn now to examine her as a disabled character in more detail, to see how Luke may be tapping into additional features of liminality provided by her disability, including the "utopian future" envisioned by the Hebrew prophets, in which "disability disappears," as Saul Olyan so aptly phrases it.[30]

THE BENT-OVER WOMAN AS NARRATIVE PROSTHESIS AND MATERIAL METAPHOR

In the previous chapter, I explored the Bent-Over Woman's physical condition through two theoretical lenses: medical anthropology and physiognomy. I turn now to consider the woman's condition as a "disability," and the potential narrative and metaphoric functions such a construction of her physical condition might make possible.[31] As I indicated above, David T. Mitchell and Sharon L. Snyder suggest that using disabled characters enables authors to use the tension between social and individual "registers of meaning-making," by using the liminality of the disabled body in the representational process of literature. Mitchell observes that, "because disability has served primarily as a metaphor for things gone awry with bodily and social orders (as opposed to the inherent mutability of bodies themselves). . . . [disability] is deployed in

---

30. Olyan, *Disability in the Hebrew Bible*, 85–89. Such a utopian ideal is a significant feature of Third Isaiah (Isaiah 56–66); we know that Luke is familiar with this portion of Isaiah, since it is from Isaiah 61 that Jesus will read in the synagogue in Nazareth.

31. There are a number of excellent, generally recent studies in disability and the bible that have informed my discussion in this section. See, for example, Abrams, *Judaism and Disability*; Avalos, et al., eds., *This Abled Body*; Olyan, *Disability in the Hebrew Bible*; and Schipper, *Disability Studies and the Hebrew Bible*. For a now classic study in Greco-Roman disability, see Garland, *Eye of the Beholder*.

literary narrative as a master metaphor for social ills."[32] Mitchell goes on to discuss Sophocles' use of Oedipus' lameness as an example from ancient literature in which "Sophocles' willingness to represent disability as a mode of experience-based knowledge proves a rare literary occasion . . . [such that] Oedipus' physical difference secures key components of the plot that allow the riddle of his identity to be unraveled."[33]

In their discussion of disability as "narrative prosthesis," Mitchell and Snyder also explore Antoine de Baecque's theory that the body is used as a "material metaphor" in order to make concrete that which is abstract.[34] His work addresses the cartoonists of the French Revolution, who used disabled bodies to depict the problems of a corrupt monarchy, and healthy, strong bodies to depict the ideals of democracy. Generalizing from de Baecque's argument, Mitchell and Snyder suggest, "one cannot narrate the story of a healthy body or national reform movement without the contrastive device of a disability to bear out the symbolic potency of the message."[35] One can see this principle at work when John the Baptist's disciples come to ask Jesus, "Are you the one who is to come, or are we to wait for another?" (Luke 7:19). Jesus responds by saying, "Go and tell John what you have seen and heard: The blind receive their sight, the lame walk, the lepers are cleansed, the deaf hear, the dead are raised, the poor have good news brought to them" (Luke 7:22). Here the utopian future for a restored Israel envisioned by the prophets is fulfilled in Jesus' actions that transform (erase/heal) disability. It is this "symbolic potency" of disability that leads me to suggest that Luke understands the Bent-Over Woman, not as an "historical" woman who actually encounters Jesus somewhere on his way to Jerusalem, but as a metaphor—a stand-in—for the community that gathers in the name of Jesus.

I suggested in the previous two chapters that the description of the Bent-Over Woman's initial physical condition and her subsequent experience of physical transformation "secures key components of the plot" (as Mitchell and Snyder phrase it) by describing her bodily experience, not with typical disabilities or physical conditions used metaphorically in the biblical tradition such as blindness, lameness,

32. Mitchell, "Narrative Prosthesis," 24.

33. Ibid., 26.

34. Mitchell and Snyder, *Narrative Prosthesis*, 62–64.

35. Ibid., 63–64. See Jeremy Schipper's application of this principle in Schipper, *Disability Studies and the Hebrew Bible*.

or deafness, but rather with language that engages traditions related to Israel's salvation from bondage and the promise that Israel will have an everlasting future, represented by the restoration of the throne of David's descendents.[36] By using language to describe her condition that is normally associated with the collectivity of Israel, Luke seems to be suggesting that she represents a new collectivity that is the recipient of the benefits of these promises; the identity of that new collectivity is the social group for whom he is writing.

Furthermore, her disability and its transformation seem to provide a bodily "geography" that maps the community's own experience.[37] As I have discussed above, in her body she makes real Mary's song that the lowly shall be lifted up (Luke 1:52), John the Baptist's expectation that "the crooked shall be made straight" (Luke 3:5b), and Jesus' own assertion that Isaiah's prophecy that "the captives shall be released" has been ful-filled (Luke 4:18). It is significant, I believe, that all three of these themes are uniquely Lukan in the synoptic tradition; neither Mark nor Matthew include them in their gospels. All three themes come together in Luke's larger narrative, not just in the story of the Bent-Over Woman, but spe-cifically in her bodily experience of having been bent low, of having been crooked, of having been held captive—and also of being restored to full uprightness, freedom, and participation in the public assembly.

In addition to this metaphoric function, she seems to serve a narra-tive function as well. Mitchell and Snyder suggest, "Our phrase narrative prosthesis is meant to indicate that disability has been used throughout history as a crutch upon which literary narratives lean for their represen-tational power, disruptive potentiality, and analytical insight."[38] One can see the truth of this observation when considering the New Testament literature; all the canonical gospels and the Book of Acts are filled with stories of disabilities transformed. As I suggested above in relationship to John the Baptist's question about Jesus' identity, these disabilities "cured" are signs of God's power at work in a new and different way in the words and deeds of Jesus of Nazareth—even though they also tend

---

36. One wonders also whether Luke may also have been thinking about Zechariah 12:8, in which the "'feeblest' among these shall be like David and the house of David shall be like God."

37. For an exploration of gender and bodies as geographical spaces, see McDowell, *Gender, Identity and Place.*

38. Mitchell and Snyder, *Narrative Prosthesis,* 49 (emphasis in original).

to fall within categories of disabilities that the Hebrew prophets claimed would be transformed in God's new creation.

The story of the Bent-Over Woman stands out for being different from all those other miracle and healing stories. And so I think that the story functions as a "narrative prosthesis" that enables Luke to evoke the disruptive potentiality of the community that gathers in Jesus' name. Her individual (micro) experience may well point toward the social (macro) experience of the community. Prior to her encounter with Jesus, she is bound and held captive by Satan; prior to Jesus' captivity, death, and resurrection, the community is bound and held captive by those who would not accept Jesus' teachings as authoritative.[39] Following her encounter with Jesus, she experiences the freedom of Israel at the Exodus, and also the salvation seen by Simeon at Jesus' dedication.[40] Following Jesus' captivity, death, and resurrection (in the gospel) and after Pentecost (in Acts), the community experiences the same freedom that Israel experienced when YHWH released it from bondage in Egypt, as well as the blessings that YHWH promised to those who would keep his commandments.[41] Furthermore, they receive power from the Holy Spirit to act in Jesus' name to perform the same signs and wonders that he was able to do,

39. This observation raises the question, who are the "captors" who do not accept Jesus' authority? Given the way in which the theme is used throughout Luke-Acts, one could suggest several possibilities: an alternative group within Judaism; Rome; even social conventions preventing marginalized persons from full participation in the life of the community. If Elaine Pagels's claim about the identification of Satan with intra-Jewish conflict is true, then the answer is another group within Judaism. If my suggestion that Luke is linking the Bent-Over Woman to the Judaea Capta coin is correct, then Rome is the answer. (See below for full discussions of both of these points). If my proposal that she is depicted by Luke as a full disciple is correct (see the discussion in chapter 3), then social conventions are the answer. I suspect that all of these possibilities may have been in play in Luke's imagination.

40. Luke has used a form of ἀπολύω to describe Simeon's request: "Now, release (ἀπολύεις) your slave, Master ... for my eyes have seen your salvation" (Luke 2:29a,30a; my translation). The Bent-Over Woman's experience is thus linked to Simeon and Jesus through the use of the verb ἀπολύω. Whereas she (and Simeon) will be released, Jesus will not be released from captivity, even though Pilate tries desperately—but unsuccessfully—to release (ἀπολύω) him (Luke 23: 16, 20, 22). Jesus' bondage will only be released through the intervention of God; it is God who will raise him up, God who will make him both Lord and Christ (Acts 2:32, 36; see also Peter's reference to Pilate's attempt to release Jesus in Acts 3:13).

41. The community's experience in Acts 2:44–47 and 4:32–35 parallels the blessings promised to those who keep the commandments in Deut 15:1–18—including the release of Hebrew slaves in the Sabbatical Year.

in order to spread salvation to the ends of the earth. It seems that Luke invites his audience to imagine themselves as the heirs or descendents of the liberated, empowered *communitas* he describes, which holds all things together in common (Acts 2:43–47; 4:32–37), and in which social barriers of all sorts have been overcome through the salvation wrought by God through Jesus and the Holy Spirit.

The themes collected together in the story of the Bent-Over Woman are also collected together in Acts 10:1—11:18, the encounter between Peter and Cornelius and its aftermath, which serves as the pivot point between sharing the gospel of Jesus among the Jews and the mission to the Gentiles that Paul will shortly take up full force in the remainder of Acts.[42] Peter summarizes these themes well in Acts 10: 34–48, his speech at Cornelius' house when he becomes convinced that Jesus' message is meant not just for the Jews, but for the Gentiles as well. While the vocabulary is different, the elements are similar to many we have been considering throughout this study, particularly in Acts 10:38 as Peter summarizes the God-inspired activities of Jesus: "God anointed Jesus of Nazareth with the Holy Spirit and with power; [and] he went about doing good and healing all who were oppressed by the devil, for God was with him."

Just as the Bent-Over Woman seems to collect and focus a number of themes in the gospel, so she seems to prefigure a number of themes that are explored in Luke's second volume related to the identity of, and membership in the community that gathers in Jesus' name. For example, in arguing from the lesser to the greater in supporting his actions in regard to the woman, Luke's Jesus brings to mind all those who are obligated to observe the Sabbath, including "the resident aliens" who live among the Israelites. Once these non-Jews are in view, it is not too far a step to imagine that other Gentiles may be able to participate in the life of the community; as Peter asks in Acts 10:47, "Can anyone withhold the water for baptizing these people [the members of Cornelius' household] who have received the Holy Spirit just as we have?" The story of the Bent-Over Woman thus seems designed by Luke to help negotiate issues related to identity formation within the social group for whom he is writing.

42. See the discussion of Acts 10:1—11:18 as a foundation narrative for Luke's social group in Wilson, "Urban Legends," 77–99.

THE BENT-OVER WOMAN AS SLAVE METAPHOR
FOR THE COMMUNITY

Now I return to the issue of slavery, to see how it functions metaphorically in Jewish literature, and how that functionality may have been used by Luke in depicting this encounter between Jesus and the Bent-Over Woman. In the previous chapter, I discussed the Greco-Roman romance novel, and its usage of the free woman mistaken for a slave as a possible corollary to the Bent-Over Woman. Here let me note briefly William Fitzgerald's discussion of two Greco-Roman works, the *Golden Ass* and *Psyche and Cupid*. He suggests, "Whatever the allegorical implications of these two stories as spiritual progresses, it is slavery that provides the terms through which these transformations can be imagined."[43] Does slavery provide the terms through which Luke's transformational goals in the story of the Bent-Over Woman can be imagined? Let us turn now to explore how slavery is used as a metaphor in Judaism, to see whether Luke's usage is similar.

Catherine Hezser has identified four ways in which slavery functioned metaphorically in Judaism in antiquity: religiously, socially, psychologically, and politically. Hezser begins with the religious usage of slavery as a metaphor, noting, "Various biblical personages such as patriarchs, kings, and prophets present themselves or are presented as 'slaves of God.'"[44] Although such personalities rank at the top of the social hierarchy, there is still one higher than they are: God. The source of the metaphor is related to Israel's defining foundational event: the liberation of the Israelites from slavery in Egypt by God. Part of the rationale God gives for observing the Jubilee Year, for example, is related to this event; Leviticus 25:42 reads: "For they are my servants, whom I brought out of the land of Egypt; they shall not be sold as slaves are sold."[45] We have seen this metaphorical usage already as the rationale Jesus implies for his actions toward the Bent-Over Woman on the Sabbath day: you keep the Sabbath by setting free those whom God enjoins you to release, because you also were once slaves in Egypt.

---

43. Fitzgerald, *Slavery and the Roman Literary Imagination*, 98.

44. Hezser, *Jewish Slavery in Antiquity*, 327.

45. Ibid., 328. This passage is one of the reasons that Flesher argues that the Hebrew Bible understands "Hebrew slaves" more as indentured servants than as chattel property. See his discussion in *Oxen*, et al., 18–21.

The social usage of the slave metaphor might seem to be in competition with this religious usage, at least in biblical terms. The social usage, as Hezser identifies it, is the naming of oneself as slave to another, say in the salutation of a letter, especially if one were asking someone of higher social rank for a favor.[46] The person using such language highlights the hierarchical distinctions between him- or herself, thereby attributing higher honor to the recipient. To represent oneself as the slave of another human being, however, conflicts with the biblical injunction that Hebrews (Jews) should not be sold as slaves, since God has redeemed Israel to be his own servants (Lev 25:42). Hezser suggests that the social usage "may have been adopted by Jews in post-exilic times on the basis of its common usage in the Near East" since it is absent from the Hebrew Bible.[47] Luke does not seem troubled by any conflict, however, since he uses this type of metaphorical slavery in portraying Simeon's request of God in Luke 2:29: "Master (δέσποτα), now set free (ἀπολύεις) your slave (τὸν δοῦλόν σου) in peace," another unique Lukan passage in which a form of ἀπολύω is juxtaposed with slavery and captivity.

The next metaphorical usage of slavery, which Hezser finds in Jewish writings of the Hellenistic and Roman period but not in the Hebrew Bible, is what she terms the "psychological" usage, in which one is described as enslaved to one's passions and emotions.[48] She observes, "In ancient thought indulging in pleasures and giving in to earthly desires was associated with slaves because slaves catered to their masters' pleasures and were considered to lack self-control."[49] Philo and Josephus, for example, both recommend guarding against enslavement to one's passions, as do the *Testaments of the Twelve Patriarchs*.[50] Hezser cites two examples from the Testaments, noting that in them the Stoic notion of enslavement to one's desires is contrasted to the biblical concept of God as the only master one should serve:

> For two passions contrary to God's commands enslave him, so that he is unable to obey God: they blind his soul, and he goes about in the day as though it were night. (*T. Jud.* 18:6)[51]

---

46. Hezser, *Slavery in Ancient Judaism*, 336.

47. Ibid., 337.

48. Ibid., 333.

49. Ibid.

50. Ibid., 334.

51. Cited in ibid. It is interesting to see the use of a disability to describe the effect of

> For those who are two-faced are not of God, but they are enslaved
> to their evil desires, so that they might be pleasing to Belial and to
> persons like themselves. (*T. Ash.* 3:2)[52]

By controlling one's passions, therefore, and offering obedience only
to God, one can be free spiritually, regardless of one's social status as
slave or free. This is Philo's proposal, according to Hezser, who in his
essay "Every Good Man is Free" (*Quod omnis probus liber sit*) asserts
that "Those in whom anger or desire or any other passion, or again any
insidious vice holds sway, are entirely enslaved, while all whose life is
regulated by law are free" (*Quod* 45).[53] Josephus, however, identifies
women as particularly prone to slavish passion, while men are particularly susceptible to their wives' and lovers' desires. Josephus excoriates
Cleopatra as a prime example: "In sum, nothing was enough by itself
for this extravagant woman, who was enslaved by her appetites, so that
the whole world failed to satisfy the desires of her imagination" (*Ant.*
15.91).[54] Hezser notes a distinction between Philo's and Josephus' treatment of the topic: while Philo contrasts the enslavement to passion with
the freedom of those who wisely focus on God, Josephus' criticism of
those enslaved to their passions "is based on common sense rather than
a notion of spiritual superiority."[55]

Hezser makes one other observation about the psychological usage of slavery as a metaphor: while the rabbis do not seem to have adopted the Stoic idea of enslavement to passions, Christians clearly did.[56]
In Romans, for example, Paul describes his inability to do that which
he knows is right (Rom 7:14–20): while he says that he is able through
Christ to "serve the law of God" (δουλεύω νόμῳ θεοῦ) with his mind,
he serves the law of sin (δουλεύω . . . νόμῳ ἁμαρτίας) with his body
(Rom 7:25). Building on what Paul starts, Augustine makes the cornerstone of his salvation theory the notion that human beings, since the
fall of Adam, have been "slaves to sin." Redemption from such slavery
is made possible only through one's belief in Christ, and is therefore

being enslaved in this passage.

52 Cited in ibid.

53. Cited in ibid., 335.

54. Cited in ibid. Hezser also cites Josephus' description of Mark Antony as "a slave
to his passion for Cleopatra" (*War* 1.243).

55. Heszer, *Slavery in Ancient Judaism,* 335.

56. Ibid.

available only to Christians; paradoxically, Christians remain slaves of God in Augustine's formulation—which ironically borrows heavily from Hellenistic Judaism.[57]

The final way in which slavery is used metaphorically in Judaism, according to Heszer, is politically, in order to describe Israel's status as a subject nation under the control of some imperial power, such as Babylon in the sixth century BCE, or under Roman oppression in the period of our text. Hezser observes, "The term slavery was used to describe the lack of political independence and liberty. To be a member of a subjected nation was considered as being a slave of the foreign powers, compelled to obey their orders and to show loyalty towards them. This usage of the slave metaphor was very common in the Graeco-Roman cultural context and appears in many literary texts."[58] Thus, not only Jewish sources, but also Greek authors such as Thucydides used slavery as a metaphor for political subjugation.[59] Philo and Josephus both use the metaphor in this way, Philo especially in his treatise on the legation to Gaius, where he advocates that Jews not engage in resistance to Caligula's plan to set up a statue of the emperor in the Temple, just as slaves would not be so foolish as to rebel against the master.[60] Josephus recounts the long history of the Jewish experience of subjugation to other empires and nations, but concludes that it is a temporary state, given that David and Solomon subjugated many nations in their own right; consequently, "the assumption of Jews' eternal slavehood has no basis in history and must be dismissed."[61]

In the story of the Bent-Over Woman, I would suggest that Luke is relying on a combination of the political and social metaphorical power of slavery, with the addition of Jesus (the "Lord") standing in for God in the religious sense. I do not see any sense of the psychological metaphorical notion of slavery; in fact, as I discussed in chapter 3, Luke seems carefully to avoid that idea in the way in which he uses the term ἀσθένεια throughout the gospel. Furthermore, as many scholars have

57. Ibid., 335–36.

58. Ibid., 341

59. Ibid.

60. Ibid., 342. Hezser suggests that Philo may have advocated this strategy as way to preserve Jewish civil rights in Alexandria, which was the goal of the legation to Caligula.

61. Ibid., 343–44.

noted,[62] Luke seems to avoid laying on Rome any blame for Jesus' death. However, the use of slavery as a political metaphor for the condition of peoples who are subject to the Roman Imperium makes one wonder whether Luke might perhaps be using a bit of "heretical subversion" (in Pierre Bourdieu's terms) related to his social group's experience as a subject people who are part of the Roman Empire. As he describes this encounter between the Bent-Over (enslaved) Woman and Jesus, does he perhaps assume his audience will be reminded of the coinage minted by Vespasian, Titus, and Domitian in the wake of the destruction of the Temple and Jerusalem that was known as "Judaea Capta," in which Israel is usually depicted as a solitary woman bound and sitting on the ground, with the Roman Empire depicted as a man standing victorious over her?[63] David Stern, in his discussion of the rabbinical use of the "Captive Woman" theme derived from Deuteronomy 21:10–14, notes that "the captive woman was not only a historical reality insofar as Jewish women were concerned; she was also an allegorical icon used by the Romans to represent the defeated Jewish nation."[64]

Is this image of a Jewish woman who "stands in" for her captive people, ubiquitous throughout the Roman Empire on these coins of various denominations during the reigns of at least 3 emperors, being subverted by Luke in his story of the (Jewish) daughter of Abraham who, held captive for eighteen years (since the destruction of Jerusalem, perhaps?), is released from captivity through her interaction with Jesus, the true "κύριος" (Lord/Master) of the descendents of Abraham? In doing so, is Luke hoping to "sever the adherence to the world of common sense by publicly proclaiming a break with the ordinary order" as Bourdieu describes the impact of heretical discourse?[65]

---

62. See, e.g., D'Angelo's discussion about Luke making Christianity "safe" for the empire in D'Angelo, "Women in Luke-Acts," 448 and *passim*, and Elaine Pagels's discussion of blaming "intimate enemies" (other Jews) rather than Rome for Jesus' death in Pagels, "Social History of Satan, Part II," 37–40, passim.

63. On the use of Roman coins for propaganda purposes in the Roman Empire see West, "Imperial Publicity on Coins of the Roman Emperors," 19–26. See the picture of a Judaea Capta coin minted by Vespasian, ibid., 21. A Google Images search on 4/11/2009 found more than 200 images on the web of these coins, minted in various denominations and by various emperors. See also. Bond, "The Coinage of the Early Roman Empire," 149–59.

64. Stern, "Captive Woman," 102.

65. Bourdieu, *Language and Symbolic Power*, 129.

Bourdieu also says concerning heretical subversion that it "exploits the possibility of changing the social world by changing the representation of this world ... by counterposing a paradoxical pre-vision, a utopia, a project, or a programme, to the ordinary vision which apprehends the social world as a natural world."[66] Thus by speaking the possibility of an alternative world aloud, what was thought to be "the way the world is" becomes simply one choice among many—thereby making it conceivable that another "world" could be produced by the collective will of the social group who recognizes that the world can be changed. Is the story of the Bent-Over Woman designed by Luke to function in such a way that it offers a "paradoxical pre-vision" of Roman power overturned? Will such heretical discourse help to speak into being the possibility of imagining—or even creating—a liberated community that gathers in the name of the "king" (Luke's redaction of Mark's "the one" who enters Jerusalem triumphantly on a donkey at Luke 19:38) who has freed it from oppression? I leave this tantalizing question in the air as we turn now to consider whom it is who has enslaved the Bent-Over Woman.

Satan as Oppressor

Luke names Satan as the slaveholder from whom Jesus sets free the Bent-Over Woman, just as God set free the Israelites from their Egyptian bondage under Pharaoh. Only here is Satan described as a captor of a human being, which seems to be unique to Luke among the writers of the New Testament. Luke's description of the woman as bound by Satan is the third use of the term "Satan" in his gospel, the second in material that is unique to it. Luke has removed it from the temptation story, where it is present in both Mark and Q (Luke 4:1–13//Matt 4:1–11//Mark 1:12–13); instead, Luke uses ὁ διάβολος alone.[67] He does leave "Satan" in the Beelzebul controversy in which Satan's kingdom, divided against itself, cannot stand (Luke 11:14–23//Matt 12:22–30//Mark 3:22–27).

Luke has omitted the scene in which Jesus calls Peter "Satan" for rejecting his prediction of his impending death (Mark 8:31–38//Luke 9:21–27), although Luke adds Satan to Jesus' prediction of Peter's betrayal

66. Ibid., 128.

67. The King James Version of the Bible uses a variant reading for Luke 4:8 that maintains the language of Mark: "And Jesus answered and said unto him, [Get thee behind me, Satan: for] it is written, Thou shalt worship the Lord thy God, and him only shalt thou serve."

at the last supper: "Simon, Simon, behold, Satan demanded to have you (plural), that he might sift you like wheat ..." (Luke 22:31); this addition seems to foreshadow both Peter's denial as well as his "turning again" to strengthen (lead) the disciples of Jesus after Pentecost. Moreover, while in Mark this prediction by Jesus is followed immediately by the journey to the Mount of Olives, Luke inserts an additional speech by Jesus before they leave:

> And he said to them, "When I sent you out with no purse or bag or sandals, did you lack anything?" They said, "Nothing." He said to them, "But now, let him who has a purse take it, and likewise a bag. And let him who has no sword sell his mantle and buy one. For I tell you that this scripture must be fulfilled in me, 'And he was counted among the lawless'; for what is written about me has its fulfillment." And they said, "Look, Lord, here are two swords." And he said to them, "It is enough." (Luke 22:35–38)

This addition is linked to the earlier sending out of the disciples (Luke 9:1–6), and the sending out of the seventy (Luke 10:1–12). What is interesting is that the first appearance of "Satan" in material unique to Luke is in Luke 10:17–20, Jesus' response to the joyful return of these 70 disciples who had been sent out to evangelize: "I saw Satan fall from heaven like a flash of lightening. See, I have given you authority to tread on snakes and scorpions, and over all the power of the enemy; and nothing will hurt you" (Luke 10:18–19). In the story of the Bent-Over Woman, Jesus will call the woman to him as he did the disciples, and will exercise his authority over Satan by liberating the woman from the bondage in which Satan has held her captive. The other unique use of Satan by Luke is to describe him "entering into Judas" in order to initiate the betrayal of Jesus (Luke 22:3)—the opportune time, apparently, that the devil (Luke 4:13) was waiting for after Jesus successfully resisted the temptations prior to the beginning of his ministry.

In all of these uses of the term by Luke, Satan stands opposed to Jesus, which many commentators have suggested represents the "war" between the forces of evil and the forces led by Jesus.[68] Elaine Pagels has shown that the personification of Satan as an agent or rival working against God or God's people emerges during the period from 165 BCE to 100 CE in the literature of "dissident" Jewish groups who were

---

68. Pagels," Social History of Satan, Part II," 17–18. In Acts, Luke uses Satan twice, once with Peter (Acts 5:3) and once with Paul (Acts 26:18).

trying to establish the legitimacy of their patterns of group identification over against the traditional Israelite pattern.[69] Pagels suggests that
"stories of Satan proliferated in particular within those radical groups
who had, in effect, themselves turned against the rest of the Jewish community and, consequently, concluded that others had turned against
them—or (as they put it) against God."[70] In the New Testament, Pagels
finds that "while the New Testament gospels *never* identify Satan with
the Romans, they *consistently* identify him with Jesus' *Jewish* enemies."[71]
As we examine Luke's use of Satan, as well as his deletion of Satan from
a number of places in his shared sources, we see that Luke seems to fit
with Pagels' findings. In each instance in which he has used Satan, Luke
appears to be arguing something about when and how to distinguish
"us" from "them."

Thus if Pagels is correct, that the use of "Satan" to describe an ad-
versary is one way in which a dissident group within Judaism describes
those "who are not-like-us," in Jonathan Z. Smith's phrase,[72] then the
story of the Bent-Over Woman functions as a piece of a larger argument
in which Luke and his audience are defining themselves over against
another Jewish group. The complex liminality of the woman serves to
suggest, as I have argued above, that she can serve as a stand in for the
social group that gathers in Jesus' name, and that believes themselves
to be the "true" Israel. Given her gender, her condition, and the actions
which she takes in the story, in Luke's imagination the true Israel appears
to be a '*communitas*' in which social status, gender, and physical condition do not stand as barriers to full participation in the public life of the
community.[73]

CONCLUSION: THE BENT-OVER WOMAN

69. Pagels, "Intimate Enemy," 105–8.

70. Ibid., 115.

71. Pagels, "Social History of Satan, Part II," 19; emphasis in original. See, however,
my suggestion that Luke is perhaps making a reference to the power of Roman impe-
rialism (overturned!) by linking the "*Judaea Capta*" coins to his depiction of the Bent-
Over Woman.

72. Jonathan Z. Smith, "*Adde Parvum Parvo Magnus Acervus Erit*," 242.

73. The depictions of the community in Acts 2 and Acts 4 suggest that Luke is imagining the idealized post-Pentecost community of Jesus' followers as a *communitas*, in
terms of economic relationships at the very least.

AND MYTHMAKING

To close this chapter, and before considering how a contemporary social group might use the social imagination model in the next chapter, I want to return to the uses of myth I addressed in chapter 1. In particular, I want to return to Bruce Lincoln's discussion of how myth, as discourse, can be used either to maintain the established structures of society, or to destabilize them in order to create new structures. He suggests that discourse, of which myth is one form, may be used both by those in power to maintain the social order's status quo, as well as by those who are members of a society's subordinate class "in their attempts to demystify, de-legitimate, and deconstruct the established norms, institutions, and discourses that play a role in constructing their subordination."[74]

In proposing that myth is a form of discourse that is available not only to those who seek to maintain established social structures, but also to those who may seek to destabilize it, Lincoln identifies three ways in which myth can be deployed by those who are seeking to engage in social change:

1. By contesting the authority or credibility of a given myth, they reduce it to the status of history or legend, depriving it of the capacity to sustain oppressive social forms.

2. By investing a history, legend, or even a fable with authority and credibility, they elevate it to the status of myth, making it a tool that can be used to construct novel social forms.

3. By proposing novel lines of interpretation for an established myth, or modifying details in its narration, they change the nature of the sentiments (and the society) it evokes.[75]

My analysis of the Bent-Over-Woman pericope suggests that Luke clearly deploys this third strategy, developing a novel line of interpretation for established myths that are a part of the worldview of his audience, in order to evoke a different society from the one in which they find themselves. Specifically, in applying the traditions of the promises to Abraham and David and their descendents to this woman, he creates a startling reconfiguration of who can consider themselves heirs of these promises. Furthermore, in suggesting that those who oppose Jesus'

74. Lincoln, *Discourse and the Construction of Society*, 4–5.
75. Ibid., 25. Lincoln also notes that it is possible to combine the strategies, ibid., 26.

interpretation of how to observe the Sabbath are aligned with Satan, he contests more traditional interpretations of Israelite history in support of his own interpretation. Moreover, the way in which he weaves his various literary themes through the story of the Bent-Over Woman suggests that he is seeking to invest this "historical" encounter with mythic stature so that it could be used to "construct novel social forms." Thus, one can see all three of the strategies identified by Lincoln in use in this story.

Lincoln does offer a caveat about how successful such an attempt to create an alternative to the established social structure can be. He identifies three key factors that influence the effectiveness of such an attempt:

> First, there is the question of whether a disruptive discourse can gain a hearing, that is, how widely and effectively it can be propagated . . . Second, there is the question of whether the discourse is persuasive or not, which is only partially a function of its logical and ideological coherence . . . It must be stressed that persuasion . . . [is] a measure of audiences' reaction to, and interaction with, the discourse . . . Finally, there is the question of whether— and the extent to which—a discourse succeeds in calling forth a following; this ultimately depends on whether a discourse elicits those sentiments out of which new social formations can be constructed.[76]

What I find intriguing about the story of the Bent-Over Woman is the difference in "reception history" of this pericope versus so many others that are unique to Luke, from the infancy narratives to the parable of the Good Samaritan to the parable of the Prodigal Son to the words of Jesus from the cross inviting God to forgive those who have crucified him. These other stories in Luke are among the most beloved of Christian congregations, having shaped the Christian imagination for centuries about how Christianity began and what it means to be a Christian. So why doesn't the story of the Bent-Over Woman receive the same hearing? Why don't audiences find her story persuasive? Why hasn't she gathered as large a following as these other passages—at least, over time?[77]

---

76. Lincoln, *Discourse and the Construction of Society*, 8.

77. Dibelius and Conzelmann note in their commentary on the Pastoral Letters (1 & 2 Timothy and Titus) that there seems to be a suggestion that the social group to whom the author of those letters is writing knows the Acts of the Apostles, which suggests it is possible that they also know Luke. I have often wondered, if that is true, whether 1 Tim 2:8–15 is written against a faction of women within the community that took the

If, as I suspect, Luke intended her to function as a metaphor for the community that gathers in the name of Jesus, I imagine that as Christianity became more institutionalized and the role of women as leaders became more problematic to the church's acceptance in the wider world, she was easy to forget.[78] Or perhaps there are simply too many allusions requiring too much familiarity with the Greek Septuagint, so that as the church transitioned to the use of Latin, her power as a model for women's discipleship was lost in translation. Certainly, as the fascination for finding the "historical" Jesus consumed scholarship in the twentieth century, she fell short of the standard of multiple attestation (that individual pericopae are found in more than one gospel suggesting multiple oral traditions leading back to words and deeds done by the "historical" Jesus), and was consigned to the dustbin of gospel oddities.

But might she be raised again as a metaphor for the group that gathers in Jesus' name? Or might she, at the very least, spark the imagination of a social group that is trying to create alternative ways to organize their life together? Let us turn to chapter 5 and see.

Bent-Over Woman's invitation to full discipleship for women as constitutive for their own leadership. Dibelius and Conzelmann, *Pastoral Epistles*, 4.

78. For a discussion of how pagan opinion shaped Christianity's response to women, see MacDonald, *Early Christian Women and Pagan Opinion*, 1996.

5

Weaving the Tapestry of Social Imagination Today

INTRODUCTION

IN THE PREVIOUS THREE chapters, I used the Social Imagination model in a detailed examination of Luke 13:10–17, a passage in which Jesus encounters a woman in the last synagogue he will enter before he fulfills his destiny in Jerusalem. In this chapter, we will return to the present, to see how a contemporary social group could use the model in a conversation about the future direction of their community. Before moving to that exploration, however, it may be useful to summarize what we learned about the Bent-Over Woman story in the Gospel of Luke. This reflection will help us to identify the social interests that seem to be at stake for Luke's group, and how the imaginative forces at play in his storytelling have been used in the service of mythmaking in order to make different patterns of relating possible to imagine. We can then apply a similar process to a hypothetical neighborhood group that is seeking to engage in community transformation today.

As I discussed in chapter 1, Burton Mack identified several guidelines in his original presentation of the theory that would be helpful in creating a conversation on some topic of interest to a social group.[1] These guidelines are:

1. Touch on two or three of the worlds intentionally

2. Make connections between the worlds by paying attention to how they are ranked, compared, etc.

3. Acknowledge honestly the incongruity between the worlds as imagined and the worlds as experienced

---

1. Mack, "The Gospel and the Gaps," 112–13.

4. Stay within the frame of reference provided by the biblical texts, the political tradition, and the cultural or social points being addressed

5. Play the gaps with a constructive proposal in mind.

We will return to these guidelines when we meet the contemporary neighborhood group later in this chapter. However, you will also recall that in order to use the model analytically, I adapted the guidelines in the following way:

1. Identify which worlds may be in play.

2. See how the worlds are ranked or compared—does one world take precedence over another? (e.g., is the world of present experience compared negatively to the "good old days" when life was less complicated?)

3. Identify the incongruity between the worlds that is being addressed. Is the incongruity between one world and another, or is it between a world as imagined and that world as experienced by members of the community?

4. Identify how the authorities are used to bridge, explain, collapse, or otherwise make sense of the incongruity.

5. How does the author "play the gaps" to make a constructive proposal?

In using the social imagination model, my analysis of Luke 13:10–17 uncovered quite a bit of new information about the passage, different from traditional commentaries on the passage. By aligning this data with the guidelines, we should be able to draw some conclusions about the social interests and concerns Luke is seeking to address with his audience.

Guideline 1: Identify which worlds may be in play.

As I suggested in chapter 1, all four worlds of the model are visible in the way in which Luke crafts the narrative of the Bent-Over Woman. I identified a number of elements that could be explored in each of the four worlds. For example, in Luke's Mythic World I looked at:

1. Sabbath observance

2. Promises to Abraham/David

3. Exodus traditions/release from bondage

4. Sabbatical/Jubilee Years

5. Isaiah's Vision of the Restoration of Israel

In his Society World (Chapter 3), I explored these elements:

1. Physical condition

2. Slavery—real and metaphoric

3. Gender roles and expectations

4. Power in relationships (e.g., social status)

In analyzing Luke's Communal World, I proposed that the following issues were under consideration: members of the community experience being transformed from their prior condition to a new one, and believe that Jesus is the "Lord" who sets them free from their "slave" status; they are thus restored to their twin inheritances as children of Abraham and as David's descendents. Furthermore, everyone in the community is in it together, regardless of social status, physical condition, gender, or ethnicity; this enables the community to live together as a "discipleship of equals." Finally, the Culture World worked in tandem with all of the other worlds, so that Luke was able to "make sense" of his community's experience by using various cultural tools available to him, including: literary genres (e.g., διήγησις, Greco-Roman romance novels), rhetorical stratagems (e.g., elaborated *chreia*, midrash), and the cultural meanings associated with disability, gender, slavery, and liberation.

Guideline 2: See how the worlds are ranked or compared

The second guideline asks whether one world takes precedence over another, and if so, why? In the case of the Bent-Over Woman, my analysis suggested the following:

1. The Mythic World is the primary world that is being "redescribed" or rethought.

2. Elements from the Society World (slavery, etc.) are used to tweak or re-imagine the Mythic World so that it can be seen to relate to "us" and not "them."

3. In addition, the tools used to work with the elements from the Mythic World and the Society World are from the Culture World

of the group, and include literary genres, rhetorical strategies, and the use of metaphor to paint a picture of how the world could (should) be.

4. The goal seems to be to imagine the Communal World differently from the way it is imagined and/or experienced in the present.

Guideline 3: Identify the incongruity between the worlds that is being addressed.

The Social Imagination model works by making it possible to see the "gaps" between the worlds as they are imagined or idealized and how a social group actually experiences them. Such incongruity "gives rise to thought" as Jonathan Z. Smith describes the gap,[2] allowing the social group to imagine alternative responses to a given situation, or to acknowledge the discrepancies between the idealized situation and reality. In the case of the Bent-Over Woman story, there seem to be two major incongruities that Luke is addressing:

1. Incongruity 1: God makes promises to the Israelites; we're not Israelites, but we still are the beneficiaries of the promises.

2. Incongruity 2: We could be an egalitarian "*communitas*" in which gender, class, physical condition are not barriers, but instead we're hierarchical, status-conscious folks (just like the rest of society).

An alternative to this second incongruity may be that the group is, in fact, already an egalitarian *communitas,* but is experiencing pressure from the general society to conform to traditional social roles and conventions. In this case, the story serves to justify their different behavior and social arrangements by aligning themselves with the depiction of Jesus' behavior and words.

Guideline 4: How are the authorities used to bridge, explain, collapse, or otherwise make sense of the incongruity?

My analysis of the Bent-Over Woman pericope identified the following ways in which the four authorities were used to support Luke's arguments about how to account for the incongruities he is addressing:

---

2. Smith, *Map is Not Territory,* 299–300.

- Foundational texts
  - The Septuagint is alluded to throughout the passage, especially the Sabbatical and Jubilee Year legislation, as well as God's promises to Abraham and to David
  - The Septuagint offers a "back in the past" source of possible social arrangements that the group can draw upon to make meaning for themselves in a new context.
  - The Septuagint also posits an ideal future in which justice and righteousness prevail for those who obey God's commands.
- Tradition
  - We (Luke's community) see ourselves as part of three strands of tradition:
    - We understand ourselves as Abraham's children, who are as numerous as the stars and who will be blessings to the nations
    - We are David's descendents, whose throne shall be established forever
    - We are part of the Exodus tradition of liberation from bondage
- Experience
  - We seem to be living somewhere in the Jewish diaspora, given the necessary familiarity with the Septuagint that Luke's writing demands, but are a group of adherents from multiple "nationalities"
  - Alternatively, we are well grounded proselytes who are now welcoming in new gentiles and the author of Luke-Acts is trying to explain how we got to be who we are ("Once upon a time . . .")
  - The destruction of the temple and Jerusalem are clearly in the past
  - Peter and Paul are also far enough back in the past to have become figures of tradition similar to Abraham and Moses
  - Within the narrative itself, the woman experiences in her body what Jesus promises is true—that the prophecy of Isaiah is fulfilled in the here and now, and not in some far off future

□ The woman embodies a reality in which all persons—regardless of gender, social status, or condition—are able to experience the freedom that God desires for God's people

- Reason

  □ How shall we think about and make sense of our life together as followers of Jesus of Nazareth? Use the persuasive tools at our command:

  - Rhetoric, διήγησις, discourse

  - Story-telling/midrash

  - Metaphor

  - Reading/hearing/interpreting the scriptures anew in a new setting

Guideline 5: How does the author "play the gaps" to make a constructive proposal?

It seems that Luke may be playing with several gaps in the Bent-Over-Woman story in order to offer his social group some proposals about how they might arrange their communal life:

1. He plays with a gender gap in social roles by depicting this woman as a full and liberated member of the covenant community, thereby suggesting that women should participate in the community as full disciples.

2. He plays with an economic gap by his allusions to the Sabbatical Year and Jubilee Year legislation, so that the woman appears to be a precursor of the scene in Acts 2:44–45 in which "all who believed were together and had all things in common; they would sell their possessions and goods and distribute the proceeds to all, as any had need."

3. He plays with an identity gap by alluding to God's promise that the throne of David's descendents would be established forever in his description of the woman's transformation, suggesting that the body of disciples gathered in Jesus' name should consider themselves the inheritors of that promise: the restored, "true" Israel, no matter how unlike the expected Israel they might look.

4. He plays with an inclusion gap by using allusions that incorporate the gentiles in some form or fashion in every case, thereby suggesting that every person in his social group should see her- or himself as participants in this new Israel, regardless of their actual ethnic origin, social status, gender, or physical condition.

In playing these gaps, Luke addresses the aspects of social organization Mack has defined as social interests: territory, land, and ancestors are transformed through the identity gap; who does or doesn't belong is transformed through the inclusion gap; systems of exchange are transformed through his economic gap; and social status and position are transformed through his gender gap.[3] In his transformation of these interests by the way in which he tells the story of the Bent-Over Woman, Luke is revealed as a master *bricoleur* of his social group's mythic system, one who appears determined to stretch the imagination of his group so that they can work out together their questions about who they are, and what their place is in the world.[4] With Luke's example in mind, let us turn now to see how a contemporary social group might embark on a similar journey of transformation, by considering the Social Imagination model as a tool for participatory civic engagement.

SOCIAL IMAGINATION AND SOCIAL TRANSFORMATION IN THE TWENTY-FIRST CENTURY

To show how a contemporary community might use the Social Imagination model, I create a hypothetical neighborhood group in some major American city, which is seeking to make its neighborhood healthier and more sustainable. I focus on the neighborhood level because it is where people live and are most familiar with the issues and concerns that affect them directly. It is also the level at which conversation takes place in a variety of formal and informal settings, where it may be possible to influence social change initiatives. Potential formal conversational opportunities include public hearings sponsored by various local government officials and agencies; civic association, homeowner association, and tenants' rights meetings; meetings with local schools and school officials, and within various non-profit entities, from religious communities to affordable housing advocates. Informal conversation opportu-

3. Mack, *Myth and the Christian Nation*, 75.

4. Mack, *Christian Myth*, 69.

nities include the checkout line in the local grocery store, chatting with one's next-door neighbors over the backyard fence, and waiting for, or riding on public transportation.

Furthermore, the neighborhood level is the level at which residents have, or may develop networks that will support change initiatives, and where their ability to implement change may have the greatest chance for success. In addition, through the process of identifying issues and concerns, imagining possible responses, and conversing with others to expand and refine these responses, capacity within the neighborhood is built that supports the sustainability and resilience of the community to address other issues and concerns in the future.[5] My focus on the neighborhood is also informed by the principles of "asset-based" community development, which shifts the paradigm from "fixing" problems and responding to people's "needs" to releasing the capacities, skills, and assets of all persons within a given community, regardless of class or social position, for investment in the community's future.[6]

One of the tasks of those embarking on social change is to engage in critical reflection both on the present shape of the social group and on the imagined shape of the group once it has been changed. Here is the point at which persons begin to speak a new world into being. "Speaking new worlds into being" implies that conversation is a key tool for using the Social Imagination model as a discursive design for social change. As a social group seeks to address an issue of concern to it, the Social Imagination model provides the "what" of the discursive design, but conversation provides the "how." To explore this element of social change, I turn now to a model of conversation that is designed to support the creation and fleshing out of all proposed ideas, before coming to a decision on how to move forward.

---

5. The Appalachian Regional Commission's study on capacity building in Appalachia identified the following principles and goals for successful community capacity building: "1) Purposive and planned action on the part of a representative cross-section of the community; 2) the mobilization and participation of a broad, diverse coalition of citizens within a community; 3) the generation of awareness of community issues and problems, as well as a sense of commitment, common purpose, and empowerment on the part of community members; 4) The strengthening of human capital by equipping people with the skills, know-how, and creativity necessary to carry out common goals; and 5) the establishment of dense collaborative networks across agencies, organizations, and individuals." Kleiner, et al., "Evaluation of the Appalachian Regional Commission's Community Capacity-Building Projects," v.

6. Kretzmann, et al. *Building Communities from the Inside Out.*

The Idea Conversation

The Social Imagination model creates an arena within which it is possible for a social group to exercise its imagination about how their life together might be different. By creating a framework for discussion, the model provides a group with tools for analyzing the worlds in which the group currently exists, as well as imagining what the worlds might look like in their most ideal form. It is in the conversational learning space created within this arena that Michael Kahn's notion of the "barn-raising" idea conversation offers a useful methodology for engaging in meaning-making conversation, especially in recognizing that conflicting values and aspirations are likely to be part of the social change process. The metaphor of barn-raising borrows from the experience of the American frontier, in which whole communities gathered together to assist a family in building a barn or other structure on their farm. During this experience, resources were shared, the initial plan for the barn created by the family who was building the barn might be improved by the ideas, experience, and suggestions of other members of the community, and relationships were built and strengthened.[7] Kahn proposes that idea conversations can function in the same way. If persons are prepared to let their own ideas become the property of the group, and to accept others' ideas as the property of the group, then the group can make each proposed idea as rich and expansive as possible.[8]

Kahn suggests that the barn-raising idea conversation embodies Martin Buber's concept of an I-Thou relationship. "An I-Thou relationship is one in which with all my heart I allow you your freedom, and with all my heart I accept and encounter you as you are, not as I would like you to be."[9] Kahn further suggests: "In the realm of conversation, an I-Thou relationship would be one in which I neither tried to change your mind nor attempted to show you that you were wrong, but rather found my way to a genuine interest in your perspective—and to a willingness to help you grasp mine, should you be interested. From this point of view, a conversation would always have at least two goals: to increase our understanding of the topic and to improve our relationship."[10]

---

7 Kahn, *Tao of Conversation,* 18–19.

8. Ibid., 19–21.

9. Ibid., 9.

10. Ibid., 10.

The advantage in striving to use conversation in this way in a setting in which some social group is seeking to create alternative ways to respond to an issue of importance to the group, is that it encourages all members of the group to participate in developing the broadest possible range of options for the group to consider. Furthermore, it helps the group to remember that a key goal of the conversation is to maintain and strengthen their relationships, particularly if the issue under consideration is one that elicits competing, deeply held beliefs or feelings.

Kahn also uses the metaphor of a jazz jam session, in which the musicians inspire and stimulate each other, so that "what emerges is a composition that no one of the musicians could have done himself."[11] An idea conversation conducted in this way can help to flesh out potential responses that no one person could have developed on her or his own. Kahn suggests that in order for such conversations to happen, there are several key goals, principles, and attitudes that members of the group should have as they enter into conversation with one another. I have arranged them in table form in order to see them more clearly: [12]

TABLE 4: Goals, Principles, and Attitudes for Kahn's Idea Conversation

Goals	To emerge from the conversation with different ideas from those held at the beginning.
	To learn something new in the conversation.
	To collaborate on building an idea better than either person could build alone.
	To emerge from the conversation feeling good about oneself and the about the other person.
Principles	Right and wrong are not useful concepts.
	Agree and disagree are also not useful concepts.
Attitudes	Persuasion is not the goal.
	The conversers are each other's teachers.
	They are, of course, also each other's students.
	People need reinforcement, recognition, validation. When an idea is interesting or helpful, it is important to acknowledge that it is.
	Puzzlements, uncertainties, and questions are useful parts of idea conversations. Challenges are not.
	It is helpful to pay attention to everything the other person says, even though that will sometimes mean deferring one's own idea or even losing it altogether.

11. Ibid., 12.
12. Ibid., 25.

Many of these principles and attitudes go against the cultural orienta-tion of American society, in which "winning" is often seen as the most important value. In a group setting where the goal of the conversation is to create alternative futures that are just and sustainable, however, setting aside the value of "winning" support for *my* position in favor of a more collaborative and cooperative style of conversation should prove to be more helpful in achieving the group's goals. Let us turn now to see how a neighborhood group might implement the Social Imagination model in its deliberations about how to create a more just, healthy, and sustain-able community, using Kahn's idea conversation as part of a process to develop alternative patterns of relating.

SOCIAL IMAGINATION IN ACTION: A NEIGHBORHOOD IMAGINES ITS LIFE DIFFERENTLY

Let us imagine that there is a neighborhood in a major American city, which is experiencing the pressures brought on by changes in the ethnic, cultural, and socio-economic status of its residents. Long-time residents are afraid that they are being pushed out to make way for younger, richer residents, who look significantly different from the current residents in terms of ethnicity, race, class, and education. The city has designated the area for significant economic development, including a new transit mode designed to bring persons from other parts of the city to the area to partake in the nightlife, shopping, and dining opportunities that are springing up along the main business street. These newer, "upscale" businesses are replacing businesses that have catered to the needs of the predominantly poorer residents who have made up the majority of the population for many years, such as check cashing stores, culturally specific clothing stores, hair salons and barber shops, and ethnic cuisine eateries.

Construction for the new transit mode has been very disruptive to the traditional bus and automobile traffic, which has sparked conversa-tion about the situation among bus riders, and between neighbors who are faced with navigating the ever-changing traffic pattern on their way to and from their daily activities. Perspectives on the value of the changes are clearly shaped by one's social location; some of the African American male bus riders, for example, are sure that the new transit mode is "not for them." There has been increasing anger toward some of the newer (white or other ethnicity) residents who are accused of driving up rents and property values, making it increasingly difficult for persons living at or just above the poverty level, and hampered by low educational skills, to make ends meet, even if they live in the public housing complex at the end of one of the major thoroughfares in the area.

Just as the city hoped in making these investments, however, young, ethnically diverse persons are beginning to purchase homes in the area. These housing units range from stand-alone single-family dwellings to single-family row houses, to "two-up/two-down" apartment row houses. In addition, there is the public housing complex that includes apartments large enough for families (two- and three-bedroom apartments in addition to the more typical studio and one-bedroom apartments), several other low-rise apartment complexes, as well as a vacant lot that is supposedly being redeveloped into luxury condominiums. Among the amenities in the neighborhood are a number of reliable bus routes that can take persons to many of the major industries around town, and a large, recently renovated supermarket, which caters to a variety of tastes and economic classes and anchors one end of the neighborhood. The supermarket is in a mall that has a number of retail spaces available for new business ventures, especially since one of the other large retailers that offered household and other goods at low prices has gone out of business because of the economic downturn across the country. In addition, there are small stores that have been supplying the needs of the current residents for some time. There is a large daycare center, a medical office building, and a large laundromat utilized by many of the neighborhood's residents in the area, all within easy access by walking or the bus. The business district along the main street runs for approximately 10 blocks, and is a mix of small and larger retail spaces, some with upper floors available for rent as offices or residences. On the street there is also a large dance studio at which yoga and other classes are offered, and two renovated theaters, one which is a playhouse and another that showcases musical and other performances.

Clearly, this neighborhood has the potential to become the latest "place to be" section of town, following in the footsteps of two or three other locations in the city that have "gentrified" during the past decade or so. There are some downsides to the area, however; among them are pockets of drug dealing by young men in the neighborhood, and a reputation for having one of the higher murder rates in the city. There is also concern that the new school superintendent, who is making drastic management and other changes to the admittedly poorly performing public school system, will close the local elementary school, sending the children in the neighborhood to other, more far-flung locations in the city. If this happens, it will make parents' lives more difficult, as they will have to factor in a longer bus ride in the morning and afternoon for their children on the city's public transportation system, since the school's bus system only serves special needs students.

People on the bus have begun to express their concern that tensions between new residents and old may get out of hand. In their conversations they have been trying to figure out how to make real their desire for a well-maintained, safe, vibrant neighborhood that has a place for everyone—newcomers and long-term residents, old and young—regardless of ethnic background or socio-economic level. In addition to talking on the bus, they have been raising their concerns in their religious communities, and some folks have even talked to the local elected officials who represent this section of the city. Through these conversations, a coalition has been growing that is focused on finding ways to make it possible for recent and long-time residents to work together to achieve a new future that has a place in it for everyone. The coalition is made up of several civic associations in the area, the local business owners' council, members and leaders in various faith communities in the neighborhood, a tenants' rights group, representatives from the public housing complex, other interested residents, and representatives of the elected officials. The large national chain that owns the supermarket has also made it possible for the store manager, who lives in the neighborhood, to participate in coalition proceedings.

The coalition's steering group decides that the best course of action is to bring everyone together to talk about their hopes and fears, concerns, and ideas for the neighborhood. Recognizing that this could quickly degenerate into an unproductive gripe session, the group decides to try a process they learned about in a presentation given at one of the local churches. Someone from the local university had been invited to introduce the church to a conversational learning process that used a theory of the social imagination to help groups brainstorm alternative ways to organize their life together, and to flesh out the ideas constructively so that they became potential alternatives for group engagement and action. The coalition decided it sounded like an intriguing process for group deliberation, and invited the university speaker to meet with them and introduce them to the process.

One of the challenges, given the diversity of the neighborhood, was to decide on the best day and time to meet. The organizing group decided that it would be best to hold an evening session on a Tuesday at one of the local churches, which had a large fellowship hall and was near both the main bus routes and within a short walking distance of the local drug store, which made a section of its large parking lot available to participants for the evening. To make it inviting for persons to attend, the group decided to make the session a dinner meeting. The group thought that such a meeting provided a great opportunity to begin to learn about each other's cultures and backgrounds, by making the shared meal a potluck for which persons brought a dish from their childhood culture. As part of the introductions, persons would share their names and where they lived in the neighborhood, and a bit about the dish they brought— why they liked it, what the ingredients were, and any special cultural significance about the dish. If participants were unable to make such a dish because of financial or time constraints, they would still tell about the dish, and have the opportunity to contribute something financially or "in-kind" that would help defray the costs of the drinks, plates, and silverware. The organizers didn't want anyone to feel as if they couldn't contribute in some fashion to the shared group experience.

The evening arrived; the potluck buffet was bountiful and the introductions were filled with lots of aha!s and laughs as people discovered that many of the cultures represented in the room used the same ingredients to make very different types of dishes. At the tables around which people sat for dinner, the learning continued as people were invited to get to know each other better by sharing stories about their names, such as whether it was a family name, or given to them by an older sibling, or perhaps the name of a famous movie star at the time of their birth. At the conclusion of dinner, table companions were invited to introduce each other to the group as a whole, as another way of building relationships among the group.

During dinner, the woman from the university had put up eight huge pieces of butcher paper around the room. Each one had a different title, which raised the curiosity of the people in the room. The first paper, entitled "Mythic World," was followed by a sheet entitled "tradition," which was followed by a piece entitled "Communal World," followed by a sheet with "experience," on it, followed by a paper with the title, "Society World" on it, followed by piece with "reason" at the top, followed by a sheet with "Culture World" on it, and a last sheet of paper between the Culture World and Mythic World sheets that said, "foundational texts." Near where the woman was standing was a flip chart that had a diagram of a circle on it; around the circle were five points that looked like this:

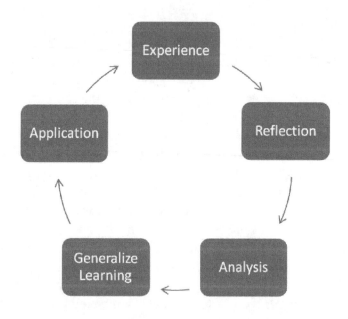

FIGURE 3: The Experiential Learning Cycle

The woman explained that the conversational learning process she was going to introduce was based on the experiential learning theory developed by David A. Kolb.[13] She said that Kolb had discovered through his research that adults, in particular, learn best when they immerse themselves in a cycle of experience and reflection that includes the opportunity to analyze an experience, generalize from that analysis, and identify potential applications that could be applied in other situations. She pointed out that they had already had a number of experiences that evening, and so invited them to do some reflecting together about the introductions and the name stories. She asked them:

13. Baker, et al., "Conversation as Experiential Learning," 52.

1. What did you experience during the introductions about the dishes?
2. What happened to the group during the introductions?
3. What do you remember from the introductions?
4. What can you apply to this neighborhood effort?

While people talked, she captured what they said on flip chart paper. Then she asked a similar set of questions about the name stories that were shared at the dinner tables:

1. What did you experience during the name stories?
2. What happened to your table group during the stories?
3. What do you remember from the stories?
4. What can you apply to this neighborhood effort?

Again, people's responses were captured on flip charts and posted at the front of the room.

The woman then went on to introduce a second component to the conversational learning process, the Social Imagination model. She explained that each sheet of butcher paper on the wall represented a component of the model, and then introduced each component briefly. She suggested that the Social Imagination model was a tool that they could use to gather information about the issues and concerns that were important to the group, as well as identify values, expectations, and possible courses of action that the neighborhood could take to achieve the goals it identified for itself.

Walking over to the sheet that had "Culture World" at the top, the woman asked the group, "What have you learned about the Culture World of the neighborhood so far tonight?" People began to name the different cultural backgrounds of others in the room. Others talked about the dishes they would have liked to prepare but couldn't, because the supermarket didn't carry the right ingredients. Others mentioned their surprise at some of the similar dishes found in cultures that they had thought were very different. Still others mentioned their surprise at finding that their name, which they had thought was unique to their culture, could be found in some form in a different culture. Pretty soon the butcher paper was almost filled up.

Then the woman walked to the other side of the room to the sheet that had "Communal World" at the top of it. Crossing out "Communal," she added "Neighborhood," and asked the group, "What have you learned about your Neighborhood World tonight?" Someone mentioned how much diversity there was, while another person mentioned that they had met neighbors who lived a block or two over that they had never spoken to before, but who worked in their same building downtown. Still others mentioned the support provided by the business owners who were there, especially the support of the national corporations that had local franchises in the neighborhood. The supermarket manager said he had a much better appreciation for his potential customer base in the neighborhood, and would look into what it would take to get some of those missing ingredients. Soon that sheet was also filled up.

The woman stopped there, and turned the meeting back over to the coalition steering group. The steering group asked the participants whether they felt this would be a useful process to continue as the neighborhood sought to understand itself better and to find ways to ensure that all persons in the neighborhood felt as if they had a stake in the neighborhood's future. Everyone agreed, and a longer meeting, to be held on Saturday in two weeks, was scheduled.

At the Saturday meeting, which was held at the same location, the woman from the university returned to facilitate, and helped the participants fill out more of the social imagination model for the neighborhood. People introduced themselves this time by going to the "foundational texts" sheet and by recording and then telling the group what 'texts' were important in shaping how they viewed the world, and why. Some of the texts were obvious, such as the Hebrew Scriptures, the Christian Bible, and the Qur'an. Others were not as obvious, such as the *Star Trek* TV series, the *Star Wars* movies, and Ayn Rand's *The Fountainhead*. A new person in the group named the Hindu *Mahabharata*, and someone else named Plato's *Republic*. The facilitator asked what surprised the group about the list. Someone mentioned that she was surprised that there were non-religious texts on the list. Someone else mentioned that he was surprised that not all of the texts were books. Someone else mentioned the diversity of religious texts that were listed.

The facilitator then asked if anybody thought there were any foundational texts that were missing. No one could see anything, so the facilitator asked, "What about the U.S. Constitution? What about the

Declaration of Independence, or Lincoln's Gettysburg Address? Don't they shape the way we view the world as Americans?" Groans and nods of assent greeted this proposal, as everyone agreed that these texts did, indeed, shape the way the people in the neighborhood understood who they were as residents of the United States. Using this revelation, the facilitator then moved over to the Mythic World sheet, and invited the participants to identify how the foundational texts informed the participants' Mythic World(s). Greeted by looks of puzzlement and confusion, the facilitator said, "Someone who's Christian, tell me what you do with what you read in the Bible." A woman in the group said, "Well, I try to save up my change during each month, and then give it to the church's 'Widow's Mite' fund to help people who knock on the church door looking for help."[14] The facilitator asked, "Where does it say to do that in the Bible?" The woman replied, "At the end of the Gospel of Matthew, Jesus says at the Last Judgment, 'I was hungry and you gave me food, I was thirsty and you gave me something to drink, I was naked and you gave me clothing.' So we try to do that at our church."[15] The facilitator asked if others could make a connection between the foundational texts they named and how they try to live it out in their daily lives. The person who mentioned *Star Trek* said Captain Picard's use of reason and diplomacy before shooting off weapons was something that he tried to practice,[16] along with the example of appreciating what each crew member, often from different species, brought to the solution of whatever problem each episode tried to resolve. The person said, "Whenever I get frustrated at work because I feel like I can't understand what's going on with my work colleagues because they do things differently than I do, I think of the crew of the Enterprise and how they managed to get along. That helps me stop, take a deep breath, and try to find another way to understand— or at least not get as frustrated!—by what my colleagues do."

14. The "Widow's Mite" refers to the woman who put two small coins into the temple offering while Jesus was teaching at the temple during the last week of his life, according to the Synoptic Gospels. Jesus described her offering as greater than the larger offerings (in monetary terms) put in by more well-to-do people because they contributed out of their abundance, while she put in all she had. See, e.g., Luke 21:1–4.

15. The story of the Last Judgment can be found in Matt 25:31–46.

16. Captain Jean-Luc Picard was the captain of the Enterprise in the *Star Trek: The Next Generation* series. All of the *Star Trek* series featured crew members from non-Earth planets.

After a few more people had shared, the facilitator asked, "What about the Constitution and the Declaration of Independence and the Gettysburg Address? What do we get from them?" A number of people began to speak all at once: "Liberty and justice for all." "Everyone is created equal." "Government of the people, by the people, for the people." "Unalienable rights." "Freedom of speech." "Freedom of religion." "Life, liberty, and the pursuit of happiness." "Freedom of Assembly." Once the torrent of phrases had slowed down, the facilitator asked, "How do these—would you call them values?—shape our world?" Someone offered, "Well, they are standards to judge our conduct by." Someone else said, "They're goals to strive for." A third person said, "They've helped us make changes over our history. Look at the abolition of slavery—late, it's true, but finally it happened. Or making it legal for women to vote—which helped to make it true that everyone is created equal, at least politically, in this country." Someone else added, "And the Civil Rights Act and the Voting Rights Act helped, too." Another person suggested, "The Clean Air Act and the Clean Water Act helped to make the environment safer for everyone, even if they were in poor communities where companies had felt they could get away with dumping toxic waste because no one would challenge them."

The facilitator said, "Great! You can see that the foundational texts—which are just tangible things—provide us with values that help us imagine an ideal world—where people aren't hungry or thirsty any more, or where all people are created equal," and she paused to put these elements on the Mythic World sheet of paper. She went on, "When our Communal World doesn't quite measure up to the ideals of our Mythic World, then we sometimes add to, or expand our interpretations of those foundational texts that helps us be better at making those standards or goals a reality," and she walked over to the tradition sheet and wrote, "Twentieth Amendment to the Constitution; Voting Rights Acts; Clean Water Act" on that sheet, along with "Widow's Mite Fund" and "Star Trek Crew."

The facilitator said, "I bet you've noticed that we haven't put anything on the Society World sheet yet." People nodded in agreement. She went on, "You remember that I said that the Society World is all about the 'real' world in which we live. I thought it would be good to really see what's in the real world out there, so I'm going to suggest that we 'exegete' the neighborhood by using a technique from Asset-Based Community

Development called 'asset mapping.'[17] We'll break into small groups of 4 or 5, and walk along various streets within this neighborhood. Take notes about what you see as you walk along—what are the businesses, government offices, open spaces, people, homes, etc., that you see? What language are signs written in? What signs are at walking eye-level? What signs are higher up, that you might read from a car or a bus? What signs are on the buses? What does that tell you about who comes into and through the neighborhood? What organizations are present in the neighborhood, such as faith communities, banks, non-profits, libraries, etc.? What kinds of facilities are there—parks? Large meeting spaces? Parking lots? Also, be sure to talk with people on the street, explain what you're doing, and ask what their hopes for the neighborhood are. We'll meet back here in an hour to collate the information we gather."

Once everyone got back from their walk through their section of the neighborhood, each group created two flip charts to summarize their findings. On the one labeled "Assets in the Neighborhood" they listed all the organizations, businesses, types of people, etc. that they had discovered. On the other chart they captured the hopes of those they had spoken to along their way. Each group was invited to put their "Assets" chart up on the wall near the Society World sheet, and their "Hopes" sheet near the Neighborhood World sheet. The group then tabulated their results, noting, for example, that the asset mapping showed that there were three major banks along the main business street, two public libraries on different streets, six faith communities, and five hair salons. From their analysis of the "Hopes" charts, they found that people's hopes seem to cluster in two primary areas: community development that would not push long-time residents out of the neighborhood if they didn't want to go, and economic options that would enable persons to support a quality life for themselves and their children.

The group was approaching the agreed-upon ending time of their session, and so the steering group of the coalition asked the participants how to proceed over the next several months. Two key ideas were developed. The first idea was to have a small group do some research into types of community development that would help to create a vibrant neighborhood while still making it possible for long-time residents to afford to stay, if they so desired; five volunteers offered to serve on this research team. The second idea was to hold a study group that would look at sources from the group's foundational texts that might help the

17. Kretzmann, et al., *Building Communities*, 6–8, passim.

group imagine some different ways of thinking about economics. After further discussion on this idea, the group decided that they would look at the concepts of the Sabbatical and Jubilee Years from the Hebrew Bible, and a story from the Gospel of Luke that seemed to focus on these concepts in some unexpected and interesting ways, in order to see how these texts might help the group develop proposals about economic options the neighborhood might implement.

With these ideas in place, the coalition summarized them in the form of two goals. The first goal was to engage in sustainable neighborhood development that would create a positive legacy for current and future generations; it was assigned to the team of volunteer researchers. The second goal was to think about economics in some new ways so that they could address the pressing economic challenges faced by residents within their community; this goal was assigned to the study group participants. The coalition members agreed that they would meet again in six weeks to hear about the findings of the research team, and the report of the study group.

Goal One: Sustainable Neighborhood Development

The neighborhood research team discovered that the sustainability of development efforts has been a concern in the developing world for nearly four decades, as international development agencies began to move away from large, high-technology development projects that were increasingly seen to be unsustainable to smaller, "low-tech" projects that were more aligned with community resources and capacities, and therefore presumed to be sustainable over the long term. As early as 1972, Robert S. McNamara, then President of the World Bank, noted in his address to the Bank's Board of Governors at their Fall meeting: "It is becoming increasingly clear that the critical issue within developing countries is not simply the pace of growth, but the nature of growth. The developing nations achieved an overall average annual GNP growth rate of more than the targeted 5% by the end of the sixties. But the social impact of that growth was so severely skewed, and the numbers of individuals all but passed by so absolutely immense, that the simple statistical achievement of that target was misleading."[18]

McNamara's speech pointed out that the *quality* of development is at least as important (if not more so) as the *quantity* of development,

18. Quoted in Huntington and Nelson, *No Easy Choice*, 2.

especially if the overall goal of development is to enable human beings to reach their full potential. In particular, the long-term viability of any development effort, and its ability actually to change for the better the conditions of poverty, underemployment, and inequity that the effort is trying to affect, become increasingly important aspects in judging its success. In other words, is the effort sustainable?

The neighborhood research team was also surprised to discover that sustainability is multi-dimensional. They learned that sustainable development is not simply an economic process; rather, to be truly sustainable it must also incorporate the social, political, cultural, and environmental realities of a community or society. As these additional dimensions were identified, it became clear that the need for sustainable development was not limited to the developing world. Indeed, especially when considering social and environmental concerns and the effects of globalization on the economies of both the developed and developing countries, sustainable development is an issue that concerns all of the earth's peoples.

Furthermore, as the researchers discovered, while both rural and urban communities are challenged by questions of sustainability, the foundations upon which sustainability can be built appear to be similar for both settings. The researchers also found that in addition to governmental and non-profit actors, the private sector should also consider sustainability an important component of its long-term future. As the neighborhood research team discovered, sustainable development involves common themes that are applicable in any development context, whether rural or urban, industrialized or developing, public or private:

1. Investment in people to expand and enhance their skills and capacities;

2. Taking into account the whole of life, including social, political, economic, and environmental factors;

3. Emphasizing local participation, leadership, and decision-making around development efforts;

4. Striving to include the diversity of peoples, cultures, situations, and goals present in a given development context; and

5. Planning for the long-term, rather than seeking only short-term solutions.[19]

19. The Appalachian Regional Commission is the perfect example of the need for a long-term vision. First established in 1965, in its more than 45-year history, the ARC

The researchers decided that they would recommend to the coalition of neighborhood residents that this set of themes, based on the experience of a number of actors in the Society World over a significant period of time, should serve as the criteria against which to evaluate any proposals they come up with for neighborhood development opportunities. In this way, the coalition could avoid a "trial and error" approach to engaging in community economic development that is sustainable over the long-term, benefiting from the experiences—both positive and negative—of others around the world.

GOAL TWO: ALTERNATIVE ECONOMIC RELATIONSHIPS

The second goal, to think about economics in new ways, was tackled by the study group. They recognized that looking to religious texts was a surprising way to begin an exploration of economic options, but felt that this strategy would give them the chance to explore economic issues from a very different perspective than the one advocated in many traditional economic and public policy textbooks, in which economic efficiency becomes a paramount value.[20] From the Hebrew Bible, therefore, they chose to look at the Sabbatical Year legislation calling for the forgiveness of debts and the release of debt-slaves every seven years (Exod 21:1–11; Lev 25:1–7; Deut 15:1–18). They also looked at the Jubilee Year legislation from Leviticus, which every fifty years calls for the redistribution of land, in addition to the forgiveness of debts and the release of debt slaves (Lev 25:8—26:46).

From the Christian Bible they looked at how a new reading of a passage from the Gospel of Luke might also challenge the neighborhood to imagine different economic activities and relationships beyond the consumerism inherent in the contemporary capitalist system. The passage on which they focused, the story of the Bent-Over Woman (Luke 13:10–17), seemed to be a key text for Luke, as it described, in narrative form, his social vision for his community. To see this text as an indica-

---

has been able to reduce by half the number of distressed counties under its jurisdiction. Based on its experience, it has also shifted its emphasis from large infrastructure projects (the Appalachian Development Highway System) to smaller community-based, local projects. See its more recent study evaluating the success of its community capacity building projects, Kleiner, et al., "Evaluation of the ARC's Community Capacity-Building Projects," ix and passim.

20. See, for example, Patton and Sawicki, *Basic Methods of Policy Analysis and Planning*, 12–13.

tor of Luke's social vision, they decided to apply the Social Imagination model in order to see how Luke might have engaged in a process similar to the one they were using to think about their own community. The "thick" description[21] of the text provided by their Social Imagination analysis helped them see how Luke appeared to weave the radical economic justice of the Sabbatical and Jubilee Year legislation of the Hebrew Bible into what was, on the surface, a healing text. They also learned about Luke's radical strategy of inclusiveness, in which physical condition, social status, gender, and race were apparently overturned as restrictions on the full participation of all persons in the community's life.

Some of the questions the study group had after their reflection on the biblical texts included: what was Luke's purpose in seeking agreement from his audience that this woman is a full and liberated member of the covenant community? Was he proposing a new understanding of women's participation in the community? What about the allusions to the Sabbatical Year legislation? Is this woman a precursor of the scene in Acts 2:44–45 in which "all who believed were together and had all things in common; they would sell their possessions and goods and distribute the proceeds to all, as any had need"? Is Luke also assuming that what will be in the background for his community is the final category named for whom keeping this commandment is obligatory: "the resident alien"—a category in which the Gentiles in Luke's community might see themselves?

It seemed to the study group that all of these possible social alignments were in view in this story, and that Luke was offering them to his community as a way to think about how their life together was organized. Through the story of the Bent-Over Woman, with its allusions to the Sabbatical Year legislation, the Jubilee Year, and the recognition that women and non-Jews are included in the command to keep Sabbath rest, it appeared that Luke was inviting his community to imagine a radically alternative future for themselves. The neighborhood group decided to bring these "thick" understandings of the biblical texts back to the next meeting of the coalition so that the entire neighborhood group could think about how debt and poverty enslave people even today in their community, and imagine ways in which they might make economic choices that help to alleviate people's suffering.

---

21. See Geertz, "Thick Description," 3–30.

Playing the Gaps on Behalf of Social Change

At the end of six weeks, the coalition of neighborhood residents reconvened to learn what the research team and the study group had discovered. This time the group decided to meet on a Sunday afternoon, in the community center of the Jewish synagogue. The woman from the local university was again present to help facilitate this next stage in the learning process.

After both groups had reported out, the facilitator helped the coalition members figure out how to capture their findings by putting the information on the big sheets of butcher paper that represented the component parts of the Social Imagination model. The group agreed that the information about sustainability had a place on the Society World chart, but also realized that there were parts of it that included the Culture World, such as cultural values about instant gratification versus planning for the long term. In the same way, while the study group had obviously spent time in the Mythic Worlds of Judaism and Christianity, the issues raised in the biblical texts had made them think about the banking options available to some of the neighborhood's poorer residents, who generally used paycheck cashing stores in the business district to cash their checks because they couldn't afford the minimum deposit to open a bank account—clearly an issue in the Society World.

To help them sort through these issues, the facilitator introduced the group to some guidelines for using the Social Imagination model. These guidelines were:

1. Touch on two or three of the worlds intentionally

2. Make connections between the worlds by paying attention to how they are ranked, compared, etc.

3. Acknowledge honestly the incongruity between the worlds as imagined and the worlds as experienced

4. Stay within the frame of reference provided by the biblical texts, the communal tradition, and the cultural or social points being addressed

5. Play the gaps with a constructive proposal in mind.

The neighborhood coalition realized that in order to imagine alternative economic relationships, especially in the areas of debt and poverty, they had learned quite a bit from their application of the Social Imagination model. For example, the information learned by the study group offered the coalition the radical economic vision of the Sabbatical and Jubilee Years, and the way in which Luke depicted the post-Pentecost followers of Jesus in the Acts of the Apostles living out the implications of this legislation by holding all their property in common. Quite a challenge to contemporary economic practices by the Mythic World! From the Society World, they had the criteria for sustainability developed by the research team, as well as the data collected from the asset-mapping of the neighborhood conducted earlier. They realized that the Culture World gave them the opportunity to identify, challenge, and critique cultural values related to debt and poverty that might be preventing them from developing new ideas about how to release the oppression experienced by persons who are in debt or living in poverty. And from the Communal (Neighborhood) World, they had the hopes and dreams articulated by themselves and their neighbors about what they wanted the neighborhood to be like in the future.

The facilitator invited them to take some additional steps. First, what are the connections between the worlds, and how they are ranked? Does the Society World take precedence over the Mythic World, for example? What is the relationship between the neighborhood, and other parts of the city (the Society World)? How could the coalition acknowledge honestly the incongruity among the worlds as they might imagine them ideally, and their own experience? For example, how possible do the members of the neighborhood coalition really believe it would be to institute either a Sabbatical or Jubilee Year in contemporary society generally? Would it be possible, for example, to muster the political will to change American consumption habits in order to reduce debt?

The ability to change American consumption habits over all seemed a bit too large a task to take on, and so the neighborhood coalition decided to focus on a more manageable scale and bring to bear the ideal of the Sabbatical and Jubilee Years locally. Here they challenged themselves to think about the following questions: What is the level of their own political will to imagine that it is possible to organize their economic relationships differently? Are they prepared to purchase from local small businesses as a way to ensure the economic vitality and diversity of their community, even if small local businesses are more expensive than Wal-Mart or other "big box" stores and have fewer product choices? Could they organize in the community to establish micro-credit programs to help persons move out of poverty through small business or other loans with lower interest rates than paycheck cashing places? What other possible economic interactions might they stimulate, such as barter or "community cash" in which their skills or talents are offered in exchange for someone else's skills and talents?

At this point, the facilitator from the university noted that the coalition was at the point to begin developing concrete proposals about how to make real the hopes of the neighborhood—an opportunity to "play the gaps" in order to create constructive options for action. She therefore introduced them to the methodology of the "idea conversation" as a way to build out possible courses of action as fully as possible.[22] She suggested that two important aspects of the idea conversation are to let ideas become the property of the entire group in order to make the idea as rich and expansive as possible, and to maintain and strengthen the relationships among group members through the conversation. She further suggested that the group adopt the goals, principles, and attitudes of the idea conversation as ground rules for their discussions moving forward, which the group agreed to do.[23] The facilitator reminded them that one of the challenges the group would experience as they moved into the stage of developing concrete action proposals, would be to see conflict within the group as a positive experience that would help to clarifying competing values, hopes, experiences, or values within the group.

The coalition then agreed that over the next three months, the group would meet every other week to work on identifying and fleshing out proposals that would help them create a more livable neighborhood in which everyone felt welcome. The group also decided that they would take on the leadership of these working sessions, but asked if the facilitator would be available for support if necessary, which she was delighted to be.

Coming to Collective Agreement on the Way to Move Forward

The coalition steering group did ask the facilitator to help them with one more task, which was to think through a process for coming to agreement on specific courses of action to take that would not undermine the

22. Kahn, *Tao of Conversation,* 18–21.
23. Ibid., 25.

relationship building that had taken place during the previous phases of the coalition's work. The facilitator noted that deliberating and making a decision on how to move forward was part of the final component of the Social Imagination model, reason. She suggested that the group consider the tools of policy analysis and decision making as part of their framework for coming to a decision, and introduced them to a five-step process for making policy decisions.[24]

The first step in the decision-making process is to define the issue being addressed. This step includes coming to a common understanding of what is trying to be resolved and identifying hoped-for outcomes if the issue is resolved, as well as understanding the context of the issue, from potential stakeholders who will be affected by any decision, as well as what prompted the decision to address the issue. The second step is analysis, which has two parts: the development of criteria for assessing the viability of alternatives to address the issue under consideration, as well as the development of those alternatives. The facilitator reminded the group that using the idea conversation would be an excellent way to develop the alternatives, using information gathered by applying the Social Imagination model as part of their consideration.

Once the alternatives have been developed, and assessed against the criteria that the group believes will help them achieve the desired outcomes relative to the issue at hand, then it is time to make a decision, which is the third step in the process. In preparing to decide, the facilitator encouraged the group to be sure to assess each alternative for potential long-term impacts and cascading consequences, as well as its political, ethical, and legal feasibility. While not necessarily deal-breakers, especially if the group is trying to make radical changes, being aware of these factors and planning how to address them will make the implementation of the chosen alternative much more successful. After weighing all these factors, the group should choose the alternative that is expected to meet most effectively the goals the group establishes. In addition, the facilitator encouraged the group to be intentional about specifying an agreed-upon decision rule, such as a simple majority, or two thirds, or consensus before voting—which acknowledges that making a decision means saying yes to one alternative and no to other options that may have been the favorite of some members of the group.

24. This five-step process is based on the U.S. Air Force's "Expanded Executive Decision-Making Framework."

This reality leads to the fourth step in the decision-making process: Reconciliation. This step acknowledges that not everyone may be happy with the choice selected. Hopefully, such disappointment has been mitigated by using the goals, principles, and attitudes of the idea conversation outlined above, so that as much as possible all the members of the group feel some ownership for each alternative developed. However, if some persons feel as though they did not get the alternative they felt was the best one, the group will want to see if there are ways that the interests and values of that alternative, which dissenters feel are not met by the selected alternative, might be incorporated in some fashion into the selected alternative. Ultimately, the group will need to rely on its agreed-upon decision rule as the final arbiter, if it is impossible to make such changes. If that is the result, the group will want to recognize that there is a gap between what the group as a whole has decided to move forward with, and the dissension by a portion of the group. The group will want to continue to be open to trying to bridge the gap as the implementation of the selected alternative moves forward.

The fifth and final step in the decision making process is the execution of the decision. This step is about actually putting the selected alternative into action. It includes two components: implementation of the selected alternative, and verification that the outcomes expected from its implementation are being achieved. Sometimes it is easy to forget that making a decision isn't the final step in successfully dealing with the issue that was the catalyst for the process in the first place. Making a plan for how to implement the chosen alternative can help ensure that the outcomes desired by the group are met fully. The plan should include things such as: in what order should the elements of the option be implemented? Are there legal, political, or budgetary issues that need to be resolved in order for the option to go forward? How will we communicate with the stakeholders throughout the implementation? How will we communicate with the public about what will be happening? Who is responsible for each component part of the implementation? What is the timetable for implementing each of these components?

Along with the implementation plan, the facilitator reminded the group that it is important to develop a verification plan to monitor the success of the implementation itself, as well as whether the new way of doing things is actually achieving the outcomes that were desired. The verification plan should also have a timetable, and should identify who is responsible for ensuring that each element of the plan is carried out. Implementation and verification should be seen as an iterative process, so that as the implementation plan moves forward, and the verification plan monitors its progress, opportunities are worked into the process to make adjustments to either plan as needed, in order to keep moving closer to achieving the ultimate outcome. The facilitator suggested that the group keep a very simple set of questions in mind that they return to at regular intervals: what's working? Why is it working? What do we need to do more, better, or differently to come closer to meeting our objective?[25]

The coalition steering group thought that this process would help them come to a collective agreement on how to move forward in making changes that would help their neighborhood become more just and sustainable. With that, the woman from the university wished them all success, and asked if they would keep her informed about their progress from time to time, which the steering group agreed to do.

CONCLUSION: SOCIAL IMAGINATION AS DISCURSIVE DESIGN

John Dryzek defines a discursive design as a "social institution" that brings together a number of actors to engage in the generation of ideas and proposals within a specific problem-solving context.[26] He further suggests that discursive designs explicitly take into account the collective needs, interests, and expectations of the actors, including the unambiguous involvement of citizens, rather than technical experts, in the development of policy alternatives and actions that can help to solve social problems identified by the group as of critical importance to them.[27]

As I have tried to show with my hypothetical neighborhood, the Social Imagination model can be used as a discursive design by social groups that are seeking to work together to solve a problem or address an issue of common interest to the members of the group. Moreover, the arena for imaginative reflection created by the framework of the worlds and authorities of the model can function in the same way that a public sphere does for John Keane. He suggests that a public sphere exists

25. Oakley and Krug, *Leadership Made Simple,* 109–17.

26. Dryzek, *Discursive Democracy,* 43.

27. Ibid., 129–32.

when: "Two or more individuals come together with the intention to 'interrogate' their own interactions, *and* the wider relations of social and political power within which they are always already embedded, with the goal of considering what they are doing, settle how they will live together, *and* determine how they might act collectively in response."[28] This description of a public sphere acknowledges that it is social, in that more than one person is involved in the process. It also self-consciously recognizes the "always-already" nature of the world, but is designed to open up space so that persons can consider whether how they are living now is how they prefer to live moving forward. If they are not living in their preferred way, it creates a space to consider how else they might live, as well as figure out how to act differently—together. The public sphere also functions critically—it asks questions not only about *how* the world works, but *why* it works that way. By engaging in such analysis, the public sphere performs the cognitive, political, and heretically subversive functions identified by Bourdieu as the way in which the *habitus* can be opened up for change.

John Dryzek suggests that another key characteristic of the public sphere is that it functions in a space between individuals and the state—a "no place" if you will, where possibilities can be explored, tested, and refined before they become accepted social practice.[29] This is why he suggests the public sphere is a potential discursive design for policy formation and implementation, in which citizens can propose and explore policy options without the participation of policy experts and technocrats. The Social Imagination model can be used as a tool to help social groups in such explorations, as they try to imagine their lives differently—together.

28. Quoted in Ibid., 37 (emphasis added).
29. Ibid., 40.

Afterword

THE IMPORT OF THE story of the Bent-Over Woman has grown upon me gradually over the past fifteen or so years. Initially she was simply a matter of expediency, the passage from Luke that would help to "prove" my contention in my Doctor of Ministry dissertation that across all four canonical gospels, in the stories of Jesus encountering unnamed women, the church preserved (perhaps inadvertently) the record of an alternative worldview of openness and liberation rather than the majority perspective of a worldview of self-denial and suffering. Then I was simply irritated on her behalf that Jesus' words to her tended to be misrepresented by translators and commentators as simply another healing, rather than the proclamation of liberation which they are; in protest she became the standard by which I selected the modern English translations of the presentation bibles my congregations gave to their 3rd graders as their first bible. But in the past several years, as I have lived with her daily, marveling at the care with which Luke has constructed her story, and his genius at layering so many nuances of liberation upon her poor suffering back, I have come to see her as a significant interpretive key that unlocks the rich depth and texture of Luke's message to his audience of hope and possibility, not just in the Gospel, but in the book of Acts as well.

I have also come to see her as emblematic of the challenge of implementing social change—assuming, of course, that such was part of Luke's purpose in including her. The ease with which she has been relegated to the liturgical and scholarly wilderness, so that most people have never heard of her (even though they have undoubtedly heard of the Good Samaritan or the Prodigal Son), is symptomatic of how hard it is to change the status quo, for it seems to me that that is what she attempts to do: to speak a different world into being, one in which all persons, regardless of gender, social status, or physical condition, are engaged fully in the life of the community.

As Bourdieu has noted, however, the taken-for-grantedness (*habitus*) of the world makes changing it a Herculean effort. Those who have tried to engage in organizational change—arguably a less involved project than changing an entire society—have often foundered on the hidden rocks of organizational culture, which I would describe as the organization's *habitus*. As those responsible for organizational change have discovered, unless the proposed change can be embedded in the organization's culture so that it becomes part of the taken-for-grantedness of "the way things are," it is likely that the change will ultimately fail.[1]

I have presented the Social Imagination model as a comprehensive process through which social groups can facilitate major social change. The hypothetical case study of the neighborhood group in chapter 5 is my imagination of a process I wish I'd had in my leadership toolkit when I was that new pastor I described in the Preface. If so, that congregation might have become healthy and growing while I was there, and perhaps IHCC would have found a way into financial sustainability. At the very least, in both instances we might have been more imaginative in identifying potential options for change.

Let me also suggest that using the Social Imagination model become part of a social group's regular practice, for world maintenance is as critical a task as world construction. Any social formation is always in a constant state of flux; adjustments and adjudications are constantly taking place to maintain the agreed-upon contours of the world. By engaging in conversation regularly that draws upon the resources of the Social Imagination model, a social group will be able to ground its adjustments in the symbol systems they hold in common. Ultimately, as John Dryzek has suggested about the public sphere,[2] the conversational arena created by the Social Imagination model is a space between individuals and the state—a "no place" aligned with Ricoeur's tensive gap between ideology and utopia, where possibilities for social action on behalf of healthy, just, and sustainable communities can be explored, tested, and refined before they become accepted social practice. Hopefully in that arena, the Bent-Over Woman can be a sign and symbol of what it is possible to imagine—and in the imagining, make it possible to do.

---

1. See John Kotter, *Leading Change*.
2. Dryzek, *Discursive Democracy*, 40.

Bibliography

"Appendix 2: An Expanded Executive Decision-Making Framework." Edited by Col Charles F. Murray. 6th ed., A-2-1-A-2-5. Newport, RI: U.S. Naval War College, 2002. Online: http://www.nwc.navy.mil/nsdm/nsdmedm2.htm.

"Gospel of Thomas." In *The Complete Gospels: Annotated Scholars Version*. Translated by Stephen J. Patterson and Marvin Meyer, edited by Robert J. Miller, 432. Sonoma, CA: Polebridge, 1992.

Abrams, Judith Z. *Judaism and Disability: Portrayals in Ancient Texts from the Tanach through the Bavli*. Washington, DC: Gallaudet University Press, 1998.

Adams, Karin. "Metaphor and Dissonance: A Reinterpretation of Hosea 4:13–14." *Journal of Biblical Literature* 127 (2008) 291–305.

Aristophanes, Jeffrey Henderson, Aristophanes, and Aristophanes. *Frogs; Assemblywomen; Wealth*. Aristophanes. [Frogs.]. Vol. 180. Cambridge: Harvard University Press, 2002.

Aristotle and H. Rackham. *Politics*. Loeb Classical Library. Rev ed. Vol. 21. Cambridge: Harvard University Press, 2005, 1932.

Arlandson, James Malcolm. *Women, Class, and Society in Early Christianity: Models from Luke-Acts*. Peabody, MA: Hendrickson, 1997.

Arndt, William, Walter Bauer, and Frederick W. Danker. *A Greek-English Lexicon of the New Testament and Other Early Christian Literature*. 3rd ed. Chicago: University of Chicago Press, 2000.

Attenborough, Richard, director. *Gandhi*. Culver City, CA: Sony Pictures Home Entertainment, 2007.

Aune, David Edward. *The New Testament in Its Literary Environment*. Library of Early Christianity 8. Philadelphia: Westminster, 1987.

Avalos, Hector, Sarah J. Melcher, and Jeremy Schipper, editors. *This Abled Body: Rethinking Disabilities in Biblical Studies*. Semeia Studies 55. Atlanta: Society of Biblical Literature, 2007.

Baker, Ann C., Patricia J. Jensen, and David A. Kolb. "Conversation as Experiential Learning." *Management Learning* 36 (2005) 411–27.

Balch, David L., and Carolyn Osiek. *Early Christian Families in Context: An Interdisciplinary Dialogue*. Religion, Marriage, and Family. Grand Rapids: Eerdmans, 2003.

Beavis, Mary Ann. "Ancient Slavery as an Interpretive Context for the New Testament Servant Parables with Special Reference to the Unjust Steward (Luke 16:1–8)." *Journal of Biblical Literature* 111 (1992) 37–54.

————. "Christian Origins, Egalitarianism, and Utopia." *Journal of Feminist Studies in Religion* 23.2 (2007) 27–49.

Berger, Peter L. *The Sacred Canopy; Elements of a Sociological Theory of Religion*. 1st ed. Garden City, NY: Doubleday, 1967.

Bergren, Ann. *Weaving Truth: Essays on Language and the Female in Greek Thought.* Hellenic Studies 19. Cambridge: Center for Hellenic Studies, Harvard University Press, 2008.

Bond, Shelagh M. "The Coinage of the Early Roman Empire." *Greece & Rome* 4 (1957) 149–59.

Bourdieu, Pierre. *Language and Symbolic Power.* Translated by Gino Raymond and Matthew Adamson. Cambridge: Harvard University Press, 1991.

———. *The Logic of Practice.* Translated by Richard Nice. Stanford: Stanford University Press, 1990.

Braun, Willi. "Body, Character and the Problem of Femaleness in Early Christian Discourse." *Religion & Theology/Religie & Teologie* 9.1–2 (2002) 108–17.

———. *Feasting and Social Rhetoric in Luke 14.* Society for New Testament Studies Monograph Series 85. New York: Cambridge University Press, 1995.

———. "The Use of Mediterranean Banquet Traditions in Luke 14:1–24." PhD diss., University of Toronto, 1993.

Brenton, Lancelot Charles Lee. *The Septuagint with Apocrypha: Greek and English.* 1851. Reprint, Peabody, MA: Hendrickson, 1986.

Bridges, William. *Managing Transitions: Making the Most of Change.* Cambridge, MA: Perseus, 2003.

Brooten, Bernadette J. *Women Leaders in the Ancient Synagogue: Inscriptional Evidence and Background Issues.* Brown Judaic Studies 36. Chico, CA: Scholars, 1982.

Brueggemann, Walter. *Finally Comes the Poet: Daring Speech for Proclamation.* Minneapolis: Fortress, 1989.

———. *The Prophetic Imagination.* 2nd ed. Minneapolis: Fortress, 2001.

———. "Restlessness and Greed: Obedience and Missional Imagination." In *Finally Comes the Poet: Daring Speech for Proclamation,* 79–110. Minneapolis: Fortress, 1989.

Bultmann, Rudolf Karl. *The History of the Synoptic Tradition.* Translated by John Marsh. Rev ed. New York: Harper & Row, 1968; 1963.

Byrne, Ruth M. J. *The Rational Imagination: How People Create Alternatives to Reality.* Cambridge: MIT Press, 2005.

Callahan, Allen Dwight, Richard A. Horsley, and Abraham Smith. "Introduction: The Slavery of New Testament Studies." In *Slavery in Text and Interpretation; Semeia Studies,* edited by Allen Dwight Callahan, Richard A. Horsley and Abraham Smith. Vol. 83/84. Atlanta: Society of Biblical Literature, 1998.

———. *Slavery in Text and Interpretation.* Semeia Studies. Vol. 83/84. Atlanta: Society of Biblical Literature, 1998.

Callaway, Mary. *Sing, O Barren One: A Study in Comparative Midrash.* Dissertation Series / Society of Biblical Literature. Vol. 91. Atlanta: Scholars Press, 1986.

Charlesworth, James H. *The Messiah: Developments in Earliest Judaism and Christianity.* Minneapolis: Fortress, 1992.

Chirichigno, Gregory. *Debt-Slavery in Israel and the Ancient Near East.* Journal for the Study of the Old Testament Supplement Series 141. Sheffield, UK: JSOT Press. 1993.

Corley, Kathleen E. "The Anointing of Jesus in the Synoptic Tradition: An Argument for Authenticity." *Journal for the Study of the Historical Jesus* 1 (2003) 61–72.

Dahl, Nils A. "The Story of Abraham in Luke-Acts." In *Studies in Luke-Acts*, edited by Leander E. Keck, Paul Schubert and J. Louis Martyn. 1966. Reprinted, Philadelphia: Fortress, 1980.

D'Angelo, Mary Rose. "Women in Luke-Acts: A Redactional View." *Journal of Biblical Literature* 109 (1990) 441–61.

Dibelius, Martin, and Hans Conzelmann. *The Pastoral Epistles; a Commentary on the Pastoral Epistles.* Hermeneia. Philadelphia: Fortress, 1972.

Doniger, Wendy. *The Implied Spider: Politics & Theology in Myth.* Lectures on the History of Religions 16. New York: Columbia University Press, 1998.

Douglas, Mary. *Purity and Danger: An Analysis of Concepts of Pollution and Taboo.* London: Routledge & Kegan Paul, 1966.

Dreifuss, Gustav. "The Figures of Satan and Abraham (in the Legends on Genesis 22. the Akedah)." *Journal of Analytical Psychology* 17.2 (1972) 166–79.

Dryzek, John S. *Discursive Democracy: Politics, Policy, and Political Science.* New York: Cambridge University Press, 1994; 1990.

DuBois, Page. *Slaves and Other Objects.* Chicago: University of Chicago Press, 2003.

Edwards, Martha Lynn. "Physical Disability in the Ancient Greek World." PhD diss., University of Minnesota, 1995.

Eusebius, G. A. Williamson, and Andrew Louth. *The History of the Church from Christ to Constantine.* Penguin Classics. Rev ed. New York: Viking Penguin, 1989.

Evans, C. F. "The Central Section of St. Luke's Gospel." In *Studies in the Gospels; Essays in Memory of R. H. Lightfoot*, edited by D. E. Nineham, 37–53. Oxford: Blackwell, 1955.

Evans, Craig A. and James A. Sanders. *Luke and Scripture: The Function of Sacred Tradition in Luke-Acts.* Minneapolis: Fortress, 1993.

Fitzgerald, William. *Slavery and the Roman Literary Imagination.* Roman Literature and Its Contexts. New York: Cambridge University Press, 2000.

Fitzmyer, Joseph A. *The Gospel According to Luke X–XX: Introduction, Translation, and Notes.* The Anchor Bible. Vol. 28A. Garden City, NY: Doubleday, 1985.

Flesher, Paul Virgil McCracken. *Oxen, Women Or Citizens? Slaves in the System of the Mishnah.* Brown Judaic Studies 143. Atlanta: Scholars, 1988.

Garland, Robert. *The Eye of the Beholder: Deformity and Disability in the Graeco-Roman World.* Ithaca, NY: Cornell University Press, 1995.

Geertz, Clifford. "Thick Description: Toward an Interpretive Theory of Culture." In *The Interpretation of Cultures; Selected Essays*, 3–30. New York: Basic Books, 1973.

Glancy, Jennifer A. *Slavery in Early Christianity.* 2002. Reprint, Minneapolis: Fortress, 2006.

Green, Joel B. "Jesus and a Daughter of Abraham (Luke 13:10–17): Test Case for a Lucan Perspective on Jesus' Miracles." *Catholic Biblical Quarterly* 51 (1989) 643–54.

Greenspahn, Frederick E., Earle Hilgert, and Burton L. Mack. *Nourished with Peace: Studies in Hellenistic Judaism in Memory of Samuel Sandmel.* Homage Series. Chico, CA: Scholars, 1984.

Hamm, M. Dennis. "The Freeing of the Bent Woman and the Restoration of Israel: Luke 13:10–17 as Narrative Theology." *Journal for the Study of the New Testament* 31 (1987) 23–44.

Harrill, James Albert. *Slaves in the New Testament: Literary, Social, and Moral Dimensions.* Minneapolis: Fortress, 2006.

Hatch, Edwin, and Henry A. Redpath. *A Concordance to the Septuagint and the Other Greek Versions of the Old Testament (Including the Apocryphal Books).* 2nd ed. Grand Rapids: Baker, 1998.

Hezser, Catherine. *Jewish Slavery in Antiquity.* Oxford: Oxford University Press, 2005.

Hodge, Caroline Johnson. *If Sons, Then Heirs: A Study of Kinship and Ethnicity in the Letters of Paul.* New York: Oxford University Press, 2007.

Horsley, Richard A. "The Slave Systems of Classical Antiquity and their Reluctant Recognition by Modern Scholars." *Semeia 83/84: Slavery in Text and Interpretation,* edited by Allen Dwight Callahan, Richard A. Horsley, and Abraham Smith. Atlanta: Society of Biblical Literature, 1998.

Houghtby, Natalie K. "Living Beyond the Horizon: Opening the Church to the Baby Boom Generation." DMin diss., School of Theology at Claremont, 1993.

Houghtby-Haddon, Natalie. "Changed Imagination, Changed Obedience: The Bent-Over Woman as Social Vision in the Gospel of Luke." PhD diss., The George Washington University, 2009.

Houghtby-Haddon, Natalie K. "The Body as Subject." Paper presented at the Mid–Atlantic Region of the American Academy of Religion. Baltimore, March 2006.

Huntington, Samuel P., and Joan M. Nelson. *No Easy Choice: Political Participation in Developing Countries.* Harvard University Center for International Affairs. Cambridge: Harvard University Press, 1976.

Josephus, Flavius. *Josephus in Nine Volumes.* Edited by H. St J. Thackeray, Ralph Marcus, Allen Paul Wikgren, Louis H. Feldman. Loeb Classical Library. Cambridge: Harvard University Press, 1976.

Joshel, Sandra R., and Sheila Murnaghan. *Women and Slaves in Greco-Roman Culture: Differential Equations.* New York: Routledge, 1998.

Kahn, Michael. *The Tao of Conversation.* Oakland, CA: New Harbinger, 1995.

Karris, Robert J. "Women and Discipleship in Luke." *Catholic Biblical Quarterly* 56 (1994) 1–20.

Keck, Leander E., Paul Schubert, and J. Louis Martyn, editors. *Studies in Luke-Acts.* 1966. Reprint, Philadelphia: Fortress, 1980.

Kennedy, George Alexander. *Progymnasmata: Greek Textbooks of Prose Composition and Rhetoric.* Writings from the Greco-Roman World 10. Atlanta: Society of Biblical Literature, 2003.

Kirby, John T. "Aristotle on Metaphor." *American Journal of Philology* 118 (1997) 517–54.

Kleiner, Brian, Kimberley Raue, Gary Silverstein, Robyn Bell, and John Wells. *Evaluation of the Appalachian Regional Commission's Capacity-Building Projects.* Washington, DC: Appalachian Regional Commission. 2004.

Kloppenborg, John S. *Q Parallels: Synopsis, Critical Notes & Concordance.* Foundations & Facets. Sonoma, CA: Polebridge, 1988.

Kolb, Alice Y., and David A. Kolb. "Learning Styles and Learning Spaces: Enhancing Experiential Learning in Higher Education." *Academy of Management Learning & Education* 4 (2005) 193–212.

Kolb, David A., Ann C. Baker, and Patricia J. Jensen. "Conversation as Experiential Learning." In *Conversational Learning: An Experiential Approach to Knowledge Creation,* 51–66. Westport, CT: Quorum, 2002.

Kotter, John P. *Leading Change.* Boston: Harvard Business School Press, 1996.

Kretzmann, John P., and John McKnight. *Building Communities from the Inside Out: A Path Toward Finding and Mobilizing a Community's Assets.* Evanston, IL; Chicago, IL: The Asset-Based Community Development Institute, Institute for Policy Research, Northwestern University; Distributed by ACTA Publications, 1993.

Lincoln, Bruce. *Discourse and the Construction of Society: Comparative Studies of Myth, Ritual, and Classification.* New York: Oxford University Press, 1989.

MacDonald, Margaret Y. *Early Christian Women and Pagan Opinion: The Power of the Hysterical Woman.* New York: Cambridge University Press, 1996.

Mack, Burton L. "The Anointing of Jesus: Elaboration within a *Chreia.*" In *Patterns of Persuasion in the Gospels,* edited by Burton L. Mack and Vernon K. Robbins, 85–106. 1989. Reprint, Eugene, OR: Wipf & Stock, 2008.

———. "Argumentation in Philo's *De Sacrificiis.*" In *The Studia Philonica Annual: Studies in Hellenistic Judaism,* edited by David T. Runia and Gregory E. Sterling. Vol. XX, 1–32. Atlanta: Society of Biblical Literature, 2008.

———. *The Christian Myth: Origins, Logic, and Legacy.* New York: Continuum, 2001.

———. "Decoding the Scriptures: Philo and the Rules of Rhetoric." In *Nourished with Peace: Studies in Hellenistic Judaism in Memory of Samuel Sandmel,* edited by Frederick E. Greenspahn, Earle Hilgert, and Burton L. Mack. Chico, CA: Scholars, 1984.

———. "Elaboration of the *Chreia* in the Hellenistic School." In *Patterns of Persuasion in the Gospels,* edited by Burton L. Mack and Vernon K. Robbins. 1989. Reprint, Eugene, OR: Wipf & Stock, 2008.

———. "The Gospel and the Gaps: A Worldly Theory of Preaching." No date.

———. *Myth and the Christian Nation: A Social Theory of Religion.* Religion in Culture. Oakville, CT: Equinox, 2008.

———. "On Redescribing Christian Origins." *Method & Theory in the Study of Religion* 8 (1996) 247–69.

———. *Rhetoric and the New Testament.* Guides to Biblical Scholarship. Minneapolis: Fortress, 1990.

Mack, Burton L., and Vernon K. Robbins. *Patterns of Persuasion in the Gospels.* 1989. Reprint, Eugene, OR: Wipf & Stock, 2008.

Mason, Steve. "Of Audience and Meaning: Reading Josephus's *Judean War* in the Context of a Flavian Audience." In *Josephus, Judea, and Christian Origins: Methods and Categories,* by Steve Mason with Michael W. Helfield, 45–68. Peabody, MA: Hendrickson, 2009.

Mason, Steve, with Michael W. Helfield. *Josephus, Judea, and Christian Origins: Methods and Categories.* Peabody, MA: Hendrickson, 2009.

McDowell, Linda. *Gender, Identity, and Place: Understanding Feminist Geographies.* Minneapolis: University of Minnesota Press, 1999.

McKay, Heather A. *Sabbath and Synagogue: The Question of Sabbath in Ancient Judaism.* Religions in the Graeco-Roman World 122. Leiden: Brill, 1994.

Miller, Robert J. *The Complete Gospels: Annotated Scholars Version.* Sonoma, CA: Polebridge, 1992.

Mitchell, David T. "Narrative Prosthesis and the Materiality of Metaphor." In *Disability Studies: Enabling the Humanities,* edited by Sharon L. Snyder, Brenda Jo Brueggemann, and Rosemarie Garland Thomson. New York: Modern Language Association of America, 2002.

Mitchell, David T., and Sharon L. Snyder. *Narrative Prosthesis: Disability and the Dependencies of Discourse.* Corporealities. Ann Arbor: University of Michigan Press, 2000.

Moxnes, Halvor. "Honor and Shame." In *The Social Sciences and New Testament Interpretation,* edited by Richard L. Rohrbaugh. Peabody, MA: Hendrickson, 1996.

Neusner, Jacob, William Scott Green, and Ernest S. Frerichs, editors. *Judaisms and Their Messiahs at the Turn of the Christian Era.* New York: Cambridge University Press, 1987.

Nineham, D. E., editor. *Studies in the Gospels; Essays in Memory of R. H. Lightfoot.* Oxford: Blackwell, 1955.

Oakley, Ed, and Doug Krug. *Leadership made Simple: Practical Solutions to Your Greatest Management Challenges.* Dallas: CornerStone Leadership Institute, 2007.

Olyan, Saul M. *Disability in the Hebrew Bible: Interpreting Mental and Physical Differences.* Cambridge: Cambridge University Press, 2008.

Osiek, Carolyn. "Female Slaves, *Porneia,* and the Limits of Obedience." In *Early Christian Families in Context: An Interdisciplinary Dialogue,* edited by David L. Balch and Carolyn Osiek, 255–74. Grand Rapids; Eerdmans, 2003.

Pagels, Elaine H. "The Social History of Satan, Part II." *Journal of the American Academy of Religion* 62 (1994) 17–58.

———. "The Social History of Satan, the 'Intimate Enemy': A Preliminary Sketch." *Harvard Theological Review* 84 (1991) 105–28.

Parsons, Mikeal Carl. *Body and Character in Luke and Acts: The Subversion of Physiognomy in Early Christianity.* Grand Rapids: Baker Academic, 2006.

Patterson, Orlando. *Slavery and Social Death: A Comparative Study.* Cambridge: Harvard University Press, 1982.

Patton, Carl V., and David S. Sawicki. *Basic Methods of Policy Analysis and Planning.* 2nd ed. Englewood Cliffs, NJ: Prentice Hall, 1993.

Philo. *Philo in Ten Volumes and Two Supplementary Volumes.* Loeb Classical Library. Translated by F. H. Colson, Ralph Marcus, and George Herbert Whitaker. Cambridge: Harvard University Press, 1968.

Pilch, John J. *Healing in the New Testament: Insights from Medical and Mediterranean Anthropology.* Minneapolis: Fortress, 2000.

Plato. *The Republic.* 12 vols. Translated by Paul Shorey. Rev. ed. Vols. 5–6. Cambridge: Harvard University Press, 1937.

Ricoeur, Paul. "The Bible and the Imagination." In *Figuring the Sacred: Religion, Narrative, and Imagination,* 144–66. Minneapolis: Fortress, 1995.

———. *Figuring the Sacred: Religion, Narrative, and Imagination.* Minneapolis: Fortress, 1995.

———. *From Text to Action.* Essays in Hermeneutics 2. Evanston, IL: Northwestern University Press, 1991.

———. "Imagination in Discourse and in Action." In *From Text to Action: Essays in Hermeneutics.* Vol. 2. Evanston, IL: Northwestern University Press, 1991.

———. "Listening to the Parables of Jesus." In *The Philosophy of Paul Rioeur: An Anthology of His Work,* edited by Charles E. Reagan and David Stewart, 239–45. Boston: Beacon, 1978.

———. *The Philosophy of Paul Ricœur: An Anthology of His Work.* Edited by Charles E. Reagan, David Stewart. Boston: Beacon, 1978.

Rohrbaugh, Richard L., editor. *The Social Sciences and New Testament Interpretation.* Peabody, MA: Hendrickson, 1996.

Saller, Richard P. "Women, Slaves, and the Economy of the Roman Household." In *Early Christian Families in Context: An Interdisciplinary Dialogue,* edited by David L. Balch and Carolyn Osiek, 185–204. Grand Rapids: Eerdmans, 2003.

Sanders, James A. "From Isaiah 61 to Luke 4." In *Luke and Scripture: The Function of Sacred Tradition in Luke-Acts,* by Craig A. Evans and James A. Sanders, 46–69. Minneapolis: Fortress, 1993.

————. "Isaiah in Luke." In *Luke and Scripture: The Function of Sacred Tradition in Luke-Acts,* by Craig A. Evans and James A. Sanders, 14–25. Minneapolis: Fortress, 1993.

————. "On the Question of Method." In *Luke and Scripture: The Function of Sacred Tradition in Luke-Acts,* edited by Craig A. Evans and James A. Sanders. Minneapolis: Fortress, 1993.

Schipper, Jeremy. *Disability Studies and the Hebrew Bible: Figuring Mephibosheth in the David Story.* Library of Hebrew Bible/Old Testament Studies 441. New York: T. & T. Clark, 2006.

Schüssler Fiorenza, Elisabeth. *In Memory of Her: A Feminist Theological Reconstruction of Christian Origins.* New York: Crossroad, 1983.

————. "Jesus and the Politics of Interpretation." *Harvard Theological Review* 90 (1997) 343–58.

Seim, Turid Karlsen. *The Double Message: Patterns of Gender in Luke-Acts.* Nashville: Abingdon, 1994.

Smith, Jonathan Z. "*Adde Parvum Parvo Magnus Acervus Erit.*" In *Map is Not Territory: Studies in the History of Religions,* 240–64. Leiden: Brill, 1978.

————. "The Bare Facts of Ritual." In *Imagining Religion: From Babylon to Jonestown,* 53–65. Chicago: University of Chicago Press, 1982.

————. *Imagining Religion: From Babylon to Jonestown.* Chicago: University of Chicago Press, 1982.

————. "The Influence of Symbols on Social Change: A Place on which to Stand." In *Map is Not Territory: Studies in the History of Religions,* 129–46. Studies in Judaism in Late Antiquity 23. Leiden: Brill, 1978.

————. *Map is Not Territory: Studies in the History of Religions.* Studies in Judaism in Late Antiquity 23. Leiden: Brill, 1978.

————. "Sacred Persistence: Toward a Redescription of Canon." In *Imagining Religion: From Babylon to Jonestown,* 36–52. Chicago: University of Chicago Press, 1982.

Snyder, Sharon L., Brenda Jo Brueggemann, and Rosemarie Garland Thomson, editors. *Disability Studies: Enabling the Humanities.* New York: Modern Language Association of America, 2002.

Stern, David. "The Captive Woman: Hellenization, Greco-Roman Erotic Narrative, and Rabbinic Literature." *Poetics Today* 19 (1998) 91–128.

Tannehill, Robert C. *The Narrative Unity of Luke-Acts: A Literary Interpretation.* Vol. 1: *The Gospel of Luke.* Foundations and Facets. Philadelphia: Fortress, 1986.

Taussig, Hal. *Jesus before God: The Prayer Life of the Historical Jesus.* Santa Rosa, CA: Polebridge, 1999.

Theon. "On Narrative." In *Progymnasmata: Greek Textbooks of Prose Composition and Rhetoric,* translated by George Alexander Kennedy, 28–42. Writings from the Greco-Roman World 10. Atlanta: Society of Biblical Literature, 2003.

Turner, Victor Witter. "Liminality and Communitas." In *The Ritual Process: Structure and Anti-Structure; Lewis Henry Morgan Lectures, 1966*. Ithaca, NY: Cornell University Press, 1969.

———. *The Ritual Process: Structure and Anti-Structure; Lewis Henry Morgan Lectures, 1966*. Ithaca, NY: Cornell University Press, 1969.

The United Methodist Church. "A Service of Christian Marriage II." In *The United Methodist Book of Worship*, 129–32. Nashville: Abingdon, 1992.

Ward, Ian. "Shabina Begum and the Headscarf Girls." *Journal of Gender Studies* 15 (2006) 119–31.

West, Louis C. "Imperial Publicity on Coins of the Roman Emperors." *Classical Journal* 45 (1949) 19–26.

Wiesel, Elie. *Messengers of God: Biblical Portraits and Legends*. New York: Random House, 1976.

Wills, Lawrence M. "The Depiction of Slavery in the Ancient Novel." In *Semeia 83/84: Slavery in Text and Interpretation; Semeia Studies*, edited by Allen Dwight Callahan, Richard A. Horsley and Abraham Smith, 113–32. Atlanta: Society of Biblical Literature, 1998.

Wilson, Walter T. "Urban Legends: Acts 10:1—11:18 and the Strategies of Greco-Roman Foundation Narratives." *Journal of Biblical Literature* 120 (2001) 77–99.

Xenophon. *Memorabilia and Oeconomicus*. Loeb Classical Library. Translated by E. C. Marchant. Cambridge: Harvard University Press, 1938.

Zerwick, Max, and Mary Grosvenor. *A Grammatical Analysis of the Greek New Testament*. 5th rev ed. Rome: Editrice Pontificio Istituto biblico, 1996.

Index